THE VOYAGES OF PIRATE

55,000 OCEAN MILES ON A CLASSIC SWAN

JUAN E. CORRADI

The Voyages of Pirate

55,000 Ocean Miles on a Classic Swan

Seapoint Books + Media LLC

PO Box 21, Brooklin, ME 04616

www.seapointbooks.com

Design and composition by Claire MacMaster

barefoot art graphic design

Maps drawn by Michele Gower, and labeled by Barbara Tedesco

Printed by Printworks Global Ltd., London & Hong Kong

First Edition

ISBN: 978-1-7325470-2-5

For CMS
Co-skipper and life mate

Navigamus in magno mari

FOREWORD

Most books on the sea are about a sailor, and sometimes also about a boat. But one book, the very one you are holding in your hands, is about a classic Swan!

The leading character is a Sparkman & Stephens Swan 38, the most successful sailboat ever produced by Nautor in Finland, and designed by the most advanced architectural firm of all times, presided over by the Stephens brothers, Olin and Rod. This Finnish/American synergy could not have resulted in anything other than an absolute masterpiece.

Our star is *Pirate.* As all sailboats with a high profile lineage, she has a personality, a soul, and a character of her own; nevertheless, she cannot write! That is why she "hands the pen over" to Juan, and tells him to write her story.

It is the love story of a sailboat and her owners, full of passion. Juan is a naturalized American from Argentina; his wife, Christina, is American. They were destined to be together, and one day they found *Pirate.* Something that cannot be expressed with words blossomed between them, something that brought the three of them through the storms of the North Atlantic, the freezing shores of the Baltic Sea, and the balmy bays of Greece, something that kept them indissolubly together for 20 years and 55,000 miles.

Only Juan's pen could have written this story: when he is not teaching political sociology at New York University, when he is not busy taking care of his beautiful dogs, or when he is not spending a weekend visiting a friend on the other side of the world—he gets bored; so, he decides to set sail on *Pirate* and go as far as the extreme parts of the Old World, to visit places full of history, mythological figures and old friends, or racing in a regatta from his beloved Newport to the island of Bermuda, following a route that everyone considers absurd, and leaving all speechless when he reaches the finish line, first in his class, after having sailed for nearly 100 miles westwards looking for the wind.

You should read this beautiful story. You should read it, and rejoice with *Pirate,* Juan and Christina. And you will laugh until you cry, feel the fearful emotion of facing waves as high as a two-story building, or smile tenderly when you finally realize how deeply can a man and a woman love a sailboat.

—Matteo Salamon, Founder and Administrator of Classic Swan Association

ACKNOWLEDGMENTS

Pirate had very good karma. A maestro drew her lines. His brother, also a genius, fitted and rigged her. She had generous sponsors with big hearts. Since her inception, the yacht had an attractive body and a bewitching soul. Over the years, good sailors, young and old, novices and world class, made her move. I cannot name them all for fear of missing some. Therefore, may they be thanked, and she be praised for all the blessings bestowed. She taught us good seamanship and good sea manners. On some occasions, she led me to believe in something greater than us all. I am grateful to Queene Hooper Foster and Spencer Smith for their encouragement and editorial support in the production of this book.

CONTENTS

PREFACE

Books, like ships, have the toughest armor,
the longest cruising range,
and mount the most powerful guns.

—Franklin D. Roosevelt

I like boats and I love sailing—I came to them a little late. They offered an avenue to leave behind not the vicissitudes of life, but its conceits. I had to catch up, make up for time lost. I am a cruiser that likes to race. In both cruising and racing I prefer the long-distance run to the sprint or the short leg. In the immensity of an ocean, life is humble and intense.

It seems that young people appreciate experiences over things, intangibles over "stuff," and that I find commendable; but the market offers them holidays, dinners, and other Instagrammable activities—nothing deep. Not the case on a boat well sailed to shores near and far, and for long stretches of time. Then and there experiences are deep—wonderment never ceases. On the horizon one is always young.

At the beginning is an end. "Is one of them sick?" "Are they in financial straits?" "Is the boat no longer sound?" Or simply and more directly, "I am shocked." These were some of the reactions of s/v *Pirate*'s crew and friends when they learned that after 21 years and 55,000 sea miles, we let her go.

I came to that decision in the middle of the winter in the year 2010. It had nothing to do with what people thought, and I had difficulty explaining the process to myself. I just felt it was the right thing to do. When I first told my wife, Christina, while somewhat puzzled, she assented without pressing for a rational explanation. I confess feeling a sense of joy, which some may find odd, if not perverse.

Christina and I were sound of body, mind, and purse; the boat had been refitted at considerable expense in her Finnish birthplace, and now looked like never before—the dark topsides shone, the new engine hummed reliably, the upgraded instruments worked well, the refreshed interior looked like new. We had enjoyed her in that condition already for one Baltic season, and we would still sail some 1,500 Scandinavian sea miles more before bidding her farewell. So why sell? The key to the answer, we think, is in the word *joy*—quite contrary to the words "How sad" or "It must feel bittersweet" that we have so often heard in similar circumstances.

Joy is what results when we take on a challenge. Year after year, without exception, *Pirate* had given us the opportunity to take on challenge after challenge on many seas, off many shores. To enjoy, we pitted the boat and ourselves against resistance, wrestled with it, and, in doing so, were sufficiently successful as to feel our own power growing. Resistance could come in the form of circumstances, conflicting schedules, limited funds, logistics, the raw elements of wind and sea, or of other people, both with us and against us as in all sports. Sometimes the game involved danger. Sometimes it required us to learn new skills. On some occasions sailing *Pirate* was about courage; on some other occasions it was a question of fortune or luck. On all occasions what was being tested was nerve. The resistance was never so strong nor so weak as to render the outcome a foregone conclusion. In short, *Pirate* gave us adventure.

The enemy of adventure is not misfortune but humdrum routine. We did not like the thought of bringing this adventuresome boat, fit and polished, to be a recreational daysailer in home waters. No: skipper and mate would move on to a more settled lifestyle of writing, reading, gardening, and tourist/traveling as they approach their sunset years, but the boat had to move on to more adventures on her own.

One last hurdle in this complex decision was resisting the temptation to retire with or on this boat. Our final act of sovereignty and hence joy would be to part with her at the top of her game and to the type of person we felt suited to her temperament. For that to happen we put as non-negotiable conditions of the sale that she be placed under the command of a Nordic sailor, under the Finnish flag—for the boat was built in Finland and after 36 years we had brought her to her birthplace—and ready to search new and far horizons. That was *Pirate*'s spirit (for some boats have souls) and that would be her destiny. At first we thought that such persnickety requirements could not be met and that we would, in the end, keep the boat. But the requirements were all met in a fortnight. *Pirate* sailed off. It was tough, but also deeply fulfilling.

And now a new search, a new challenge, began. We had never owned a traditional wooden yawl and it is an experience we thought we should enjoy. A friend of ours said that wooden yachts are quieter, warmer, don't sweat, and of course, they are like old houses—they have immense charm. We would look for perfection in wood in the shape of a classic boat. We found one, and different adventures followed, which are not the subject of this book.

So now, I wish to tell the story of this marvelous classic Swan—our magic carpet—and the feeling of fulfillment she gave her crews.

Pirate's Short CV

Swan 38/019 *Pirate* (116 Swan 38s were built) was sold by the sales office for USA and Canada of Nautor, Inc., in Maryland. Olin Stephens drew her lines. Production of hull No. 019 started in early 1974. The boat left the factory by truck on June 16, 1974, and was shipped from Helsinki to Boston the following day. After arrival in America she was rigged and prepared for sailing by Rod Stephens and Mitch Gibbons-Neff.

Pirate's first owner, Alan McIlhenny, raced her to Bermuda in 1976, but he did not keep her long. In 1979, she was purchased by Max Mehlburger, who raced her with great success for a decade, notably winning the Marion-Bermuda Race in 1985 (first overall and Class E) and 1987 (Class E). In 1989, I, Juan E. Corradi, acquired her, and kept her for the next 21 years. During that period she was maintained carefully and refitted extensively three times: in 1989–90, in 1994–5, and in 2007–8. She crossed the Atlantic four times, won the Cruising Division of the Newport to Bermuda Race in 1990, and was first in the St. Augustine Class of the America 500 Rally in 1992. In addition to her Atlantic crossings, she raced locally in the US, Europe and the Azores, cruised the entire Mediterranean three times, sailed the Caribbean for several seasons, spent four years in the North Sea and the Baltic, and went beyond the Arctic Circle in Norway before "going home" to be restored in Finland in 2008.

After a summer of Nordic sailing with us and her new owner, Harri Svahn, *Pirate* was delivered to Mallorca via ship, in July 2010. She sailed in the Mediterranean under the Finnish flag, renamed *Marhar*. Harri, who was not known for keeping his boats long (he had nine before) sold *Marhar* to another sailor from Helsinki, Henrik

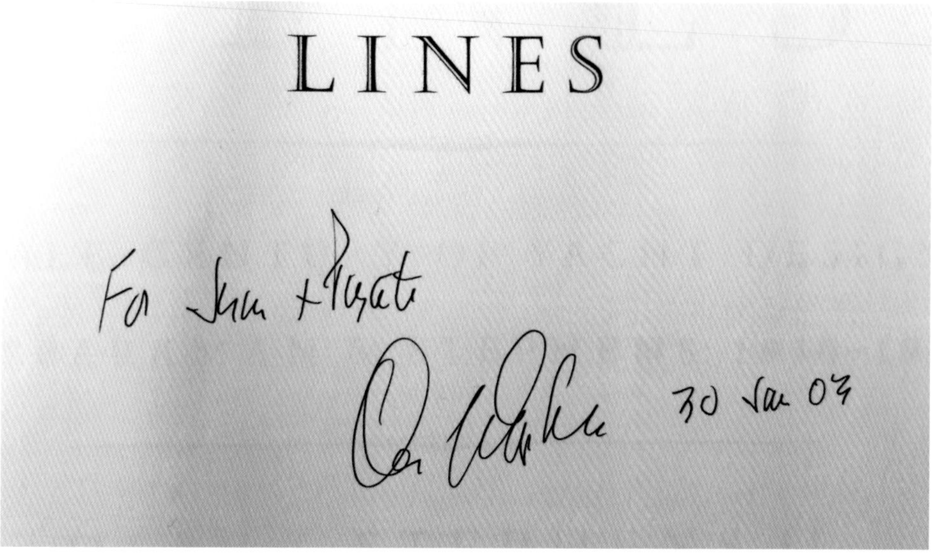

Olin Stephens dedication of his book, *Lines*, For Juan and *Pirate*

Resman, who had over twenty years of experience working in media-related business in Finland and abroad. He returned her to her original name, *Pirate*, and sailed her as a family boat in his native archipelago.

Today *Pirate* lives on as one of the many classic Swans listed and monitored by an organization formed and managed by Matteo Salamon in Milano. Matteo has produced a volume in which all classic Swans are presented, drawn, and described—including details of their remarkable technical features. The homepage can be found at www.classicswan.org. *Pirate* continues to give her owners and crews both pleasure and thrills.

In the world of swans, *Pirate*'s black hull suggests she might be the Swan of Tuonela, the mythical eternal swan of Finland's national saga *Kalevala*. Tuonela, the Kingdom of Death, the Hades of Finnish mythology, is surrounded by a broad river of black water and rapid current, on which a black swan glides in majestic fashion and sings, but hers is not the usual swan song: in the Kingdom of Death, she never dies.

A Recollection
Keeping Her Whole

Our family bought the boat early in 2015 and we re-named her right away back to her original name of Pirate. *Changing her name was obvious, as we wanted to respect her merits under her past owners. We understood her pedigree as one of those boats that were sailed and loved by her past owners. Sailing with her now for three seasons, she is already part of our family.* Pirate *is sailing in her home water in the Gulf of Finland and is doing numerous trips around the Baltics. We enjoy her sailing performance and her beauty and we are committed to preserve her for posterity.*

—Henrik Resman

1

Destination Bermuda

Every normal man must be tempted at
Times to spit on his hands,
Hoist the black flag,
And begin slitting throats.

—H.L. Mencken

Pirate heels to a freshening breeze, lee rail awash, the watch on deck alert to whim of wind and wave. The Gulf Stream is ahead. The maneuvers and techniques to handle the racing boat are part of the knowledge and skill that sailors have honed for centuries. But unlike the old sailing ships, our boat offers no gain in battle or in the fishery. All she gives us is the tang of salty spray, the sound of her taut rigging, the freedom and adventure. To early mariners it would have seemed insane: *He that would go to sea for pleasure would go to hell for a pastime.* And yet, in the hellish pastime, we have company.

Damn everything else: the Bermuda Race is on! On other boats, women and men seek the same sense of fulfillment that comes from pitting muscle and wit, brain and brawn, against the forces of nature. Medical doctors, carpenters, college students, commodity traders, workers, lawyers, bankers, teachers, have taken to the sea in state-of-the-art vessels, or old schooners and yawls, to test themselves and their boats. The hardships of preparation, the pre-race bustle, the time stolen from work and given to the passion, the effort and the expense, are behind them. The focus is on performance.

What's in a name? There is something about the word "pirate" that triggers the imagination of children and adults alike. If there is some fascination with the word, it is probably due to the notion that pirates, whether cutthroats or not, were above all free, recognizing no law but their own, and they were often loyal among themselves. Somehow *Pirate* and her crew were eager to display that spirit. They found one way to do it in offshore racing.

The keyword is "all-around." The Bermuda races are all-around tests of the skipper, the navigator, the crew, and the boat. The races are long enough, difficult enough, and unpredictable enough, to mobilize teams of human beings for several months before the event, and to demand their best during the few intense days of racing. "All-around" also means a gentlemanly endeavor. A gentleman or gentlewoman is someone who has the leisure to do several things well, but perhaps none of them too well. The definition separates amateurs from professionals in a fairly neat way. And finally, "all-around" is a reference to a certain ideal of a yacht, before specialization.

Carleton Mitchell, the winner of three consecutive Newport to Bermuda Races on the Sparkman & Stephens yawl *Finisterre*, put it clearly in an interview:

> *She had been built for this, my dream ship: to carry sail and drive hard, to go anywhere in safety and in comfort. She had to be small enough to be handled by me alone and to lie snug in tiny harbors, yet spacious enough below decks to accommodate a crew in harmony for extended periods. She must be rugged enough to cross an ocean; fast enough to be exciting to race, yet easily handled, stable, and sea-kindly. In short, she had to be a ship which had never existed and never could, in theory. I knew all too well the accepted dictum of marine design: 'Every sailing vessel must be a compromise.' And I wanted everything!*

He took this brief to Olin Stephens, and the designer came up with *Finisterre*. All-around yachtsmen, all-around boats, and an all-around race: together they constituted the nobility of the sport. Specialization, technical progress, commercial sponsorship, heightened competition, and the compression of time and space in the 21st century have relegated such old nobility to the margins of the sport.

A swashbuckling start to the Bermuda race.

Completed in 1974, *Pirate* celebrated her second, 11th, 13th, 16th, and 30th birthdays racing to Bermuda. The first race to Bermuda was skippered by Alan McIlhenny, the second and third by her second master, Max Mehlburger; the last two were under my command. She won prizes in three of the five.

In 1985, under the command of Max Mehlburger, *Pirate* won the Marion–Bermuda Race (first in a fleet of 150 yachts), which in those days allowed only traditional (non-electronic) methods of navigation. *Pirate* was the ninth boat across the finish line, and the crew knew that they had had a fast passage. (An account of *Pirate*'s feats in the Marion–Bermuda Race appeared in Mark Gabrielson's book, *Corinthian Resolve: The Story of the Marion–Bermuda Race*; Seapoint Books, NY: 2017; pages 55, 109, 100.)

They had finished at about 0700 and had to wait until evening before final results. They struggled to suppress their high hopes. The day was spent in suspense at the Royal Hamilton Amateur Dinghy Club as more boats were added to the results board. The crew was still at the RHADC when the commodore brought them a bottle of champagne and gave them the news.

For the rest of their stay in Bermuda, the proud crew wore their shirts or blazers with *Pirate* patches. The people of Bermuda seemed to really love the yacht, perhaps because of the island's history of piracy. In later years, when *Pirate* returned to reap more trophies, the islands continued to welcome her fondly, as a glorious buccaneer.

Glory was tempting. The boat and her crew had such a great time on their first victorious race that they came back again in 1987. Although not the winner overall, *Pirate* came in first in class nonetheless. Max Mehlburger, her owner and skipper, revealed some of the secrets for victory. In his transcription offered below, he said the boat should be "seasoned" like well-stored wine or aged beef. *Pirate* had indeed a seasoned hull.

Pirate came into her own as a long-distance ocean racer, and always did much better in offshore races than around the buoys. One explanation lies in the fact that ocean races are more about strategy than tactics, and that her skippers were better strategists than tacticians. Dennis Conner best described the difference:

> *Strategy we will define as sailing in response to wind, weather, and current. Strategy involves decisions aimed at getting the boat around the race course or to your next landfall quickly without regard to other boats. [...] Tactics, on the other hand, are defined more narrowly as the moves and countermoves you make to get ahead of other boats when you are racing. To put this another way: Strategy has to do primarily with the laws of nature; tactics primarily with the laws of humans, some might say the laws of the jungle.*[1]

[1] Dennis Conner and Michael Levitt, *Sail Like a Champion*; New York: St. Martin's Press, 1992; p.233.

During the ten years that Max Mehlburger cruised and raced from Maine to the Caribbean on *Pirate*, over 100 people came on board as crew. From them grew a nucleus of a team that sailed her hard, even through a hurricane. Despite the hardships, she was kept in great shape by a meticulous skipper. Mehlburger described himself as a cruising sailor at heart. He took the shiny black sloop up and down the East Coast of the United States, from New England to Florida, with long stays in Narragansett and Chesapeake Bays. Mehlburger had quite a bit of experience racing small boats inland, but his ocean experience prior to the 1985 Marion to Bermuda race was only one race from St. Petersburg in Florida to Isla Mujeres in Mexico, as navigator on a friend's 33' sloop. A lawyer in his middle age, he wanted to be a hot racing skipper before it was too late. *Pirate* obliged.

Pirate always imbued her skippers and crew with a swashbuckling spirit. On *Pirate*, one may start as a cruiser, but ends inevitably as a competitive sailor. In the 1980s, Nick Nicholson, then editor of *Practical Sailor*, was *Pirate*'s racing navigator. He was an expert measurer, knew all the technical rules, and measured boats for the America's Cup. He had long Bermuda experience, and besides editing and racing, he was completing a heavy displacement cutter that would take him around the world. *Pirate* was featured more than once in *Practical Sailor*. I met him in 1989, and he readily agreed to re-measure *Pirate* for the 1990 Bermuda Race, for as he said, he "loved the old girl."

One dawn in Narragansett Bay, as I helped Nick with freeboard and stiffness measurements while the boat floated placidly on a rippleless sea, he passed on some secrets of her performance, namely what he thought were her best points of sail. For Nick, it was like driving a stick shift car: changing sails was changing gears, quickly and at the right moment—and yes, you may skip one gear as you downshift. I grew up in Argentina riding horses with my father; as a sailor, I realized that the relationship between a boat and myself was akin to that between a rider and his horse. Boats have idiosyncrasies, like animated things, with quite specific temperaments at sea.

In the Marion to Bermuda races of the '80s, *Pirate*'s crew members did not have much offshore experience, but all of them raced nifty little boats—dinghies, Y-Flyers, and Hobie Cats. *Pirate* turned them into long-range buccaneers. Mehlburger confessed that his method of weather analysis was direct: he took the forecast seriously, and then based a radical plan upon it. Of the 1985 race he said: "If the weather forecast had been inaccurate, the finish line committee would have gone home long before we finished from our otherwise radical position 110 miles west of the rhumbline. We had intentionally positioned ourselves for the predicted weather and it paid off." He played the wind without being obsessed by the vagaries of the Gulf Stream. The skipper played big, risked big, and won big. Strategy was paramount.

In the span of *Pirate*'s life, ocean racing changed a great deal. Yacht racing went commercial. A whole new class of well-paid racing sailors sprang up. Few racing skippers own their boats. The majority are guns for hire by corporate sponsors in search of publicity. You can see them in various ports of the world: mostly young men (and a few women) with big shoulders, square chins and Mole wrench handshakes. Today the designers, the builders, and the sailmakers participate in sailing as much as the sailors. That may not be new, except in its scope and extent. Businesses and professions shape the sport more directly than ever. Competitive sailing is much more a product of computers and the chemical industry. In short, ocean racing today is an amalgam of specialized activities, performed by dedicated professionals. Designers, boatyards, hardware manufacturers, sailmakers, skippers, and crew members come together for specific projects and campaigns. Their aim is to win races and thus contribute to the commercial success of a sponsoring organization—and often to tease the obsession of a passionate billionaire.

Like so many other endeavors, ocean racing now is global. In one respect it has always been global, as shown in such extraordinary feats of seamanship as the OSTAR, the Volvo Race, or the Vendée Globe. Designers, production teams, and sailing crews are assembled from all points of the globe. There has been a long tradition of that in premier yacht racing, for example, the presence of Scandinavian crews on the America's Cup boats between 1900 and 1937. The difference today is the predominance of corporate money and highly specialized skills that are totally indifferent to nationality. One unintended, but interesting, consequence is that boats from distant and small countries are able to race in such events. In the past, ocean racing was reserved for a few people in a few rich countries. Today it is the domain of professionals in many countries. This is part of a larger sociological phenomenon: a new division between the mobile identity of people from Anywhere, and the roots-based identity of the people from Somewhere, as described by David Goodhart in *The Road to Somewhere,* (London; Hurst, 2017). The result is the substitution of cosmopolitan meritocracies for earlier parochial aristocracies. But as amateur racing fades, the romantic nobility of the sport also fades.

However, if we evaluate these developments from the standpoint of racing style, soundness of design, comfort, or beauty, and roughly what the various constituencies get out of ocean racing in relation to what they put into it, (in funds, research, and organizational effort,) then the enterprise starts looking slightly absurd. Olin Stephens suggested this in an interview by Sloan Wilson; "Olin Stephens on the State of Sailing," in *Sailing*, November 1992, p.43-44. Professional sailors make racing more vicious. Designers play cat-and-mouse games with rule makers and handicappers to produce boats that can go a fraction faster than more rational designs. Seaworthiness suffers. Also, the expense of building extreme designs grows while their usefulness shrinks. After a race or two, these extraordinary sailing machines end up in a junkyard. The lives of these boats are nasty, brutish, and short. They represent maximum effort for modest results—the 21st century version of conspicuous consumption.

For the regular people, there is a way to race in this system, even though it is skewed for the three B's of yachting: Big Egos, Big Bucks, Big Boats. Take a seasoned and seaworthy boat, sail her to her maximum potential, and play in the few conditions in which, due to the time allowances of a rule and the good design features of the boat, she can outrace her fancier rivals. *Pirate* played in the interstices and on the margins of the system, and had a great time with the game. The Bermuda Race is suited to this plan, since it is a stubborn remnant of a time when amateurs sailed their own yachts with their families and friends. In the days when classic Swans were built, racing was an extension of cruising. With such boats, one's mind is half on the race, and half on the boat. With pure racers, one goes as fast as one can, never mind the boat, which is just a surf board to glory.

In order to counteract the self-defeating trends in ocean racing, and to preserve some of the flavor and attendance of the traditional days, the Bermuda Race committee introduced a Cruising Division in the 1990 race, with the racer-cruiser in mind. The new division managed to revive the spirit of the earlier Bermuda Races. In 1990, 152 yachts headed out from Newport in search of honor and glory, which lay 638 miles away; this was a 25 percent increase on 1988. Of the 152 yachts, 34 sailed in the new Cruising Division, including Bermuda's *Tonka* and Warren Brown's *War Baby*. In the Racing Division, the longest boat was *Boomerang*, at 81 feet. In the Cruising fleet, the longest boats were *Karyatis* (70 feet), followed by *Arcadia* and *Starlight Express*, both 69 feet. Compared to these yachts, *Pirate* was a quaint little old yacht, known in Bermuda for the Marion to Bermuda victories of 1985 and 1987. The 1990 race suited her well for two good reasons. First, *Pirate*'s old One Ton design, adapted to the requirements of the IMS Rule (The International Measurement System [IMS] is a system of handicapping sailboats for the purpose of racing that replaced the earlier International Offshore Rule [IOR] system in the early 1990s), made her potentially powerful, especially to windward in heavier air. Second, she received a time allowance that faster and newer rivals would find difficult to beat. In the final analysis, luck and strategy played a large part, for we chose a course away from the fleet, and avoided boat for boat competition.

In a way the event was historic: the first Bermuda Race to include a Cruising Division. The start was 1300 hours off Brenton Reef in Newport, Rhode Island, on Friday, June 15. The finish: off St. David's Head, Bermuda. Waiting for the winners at the Royal Bermuda Yacht Club were 36 cups, plaques, tankards, and other trophies: among them, the St. David's Lighthouse Trophy, for the winner of the Racing Division; the Overall Performance Trophy for the class winner on corrected time who beats the next two boats in her class by the largest margin; the William C. Finley Trophy, for the yacht older than 15 years with the best corrected time position; the Sterling Silver Plaque for the first yacht to finish in the Racing Division; the George Mixter Trophy for the navigators of the winning yachts in both divisions; the various class trophies; and many more, including a cast iron pan for the cook of the last yacht to finish. *Pirate* was assigned to Class G. By a happy coincidence, the prize for that class was a silver cup donated by the Yacht Club Argentino. That trophy had the names of several legendary yachts of the River Plate engraved on its bowl, a river with which I was familiar.

In 1990, a new grand trophy was up for grabs in the race. The winner of the Cruising Division would receive the Royal Mail Cup, which had just been acquired by the Royal Bermuda Yacht Club. In 1938, the Royal Mail Steam Packet Company presented that cup to the Bermuda shipping agency Harnett & Richardson for their use. Following Mr. Harnett's death in 1970, the trophy was presented in his memory by his widow to the RBYC for an appropriate use. The 30-inch cup was impressive. And the very first winner would be our small sloop, a mouse that roared, a stalwart survivor of the racing-cruising days!

For me, awesome was the start of the 37th Ocean Yacht Race from Newport to Bermuda. In my hands and on my shoulders, I felt the combined force of several traditions: the prestige of a venerable race, the reputation of the boat, from the ancient Greeks, the urge to run upon the waves.

On the eve of the race, the weather forecast called for several days of wind from the southeast, as a weak low-pressure system stumbled over the course. The wind was coming directly from Bermuda. To many, the predictions suggested a rhumb line course. Most of the fleet stuck close to the rhumb line, and several wind and Gulf Stream shifts took a number of boats east of the line. The majority of the boats braced for a slow race, with the wind close on the nose. My options were two: follow the weather predictions, sail with the herd along the rhumb line, and push the boat the best I could, with frequent tacks; or go west, the conventional Bermuda Race wisdom—which in this case seemed like a radical gamble.

I remembered *Pirate*'s past victories in the Marion to Bermuda Race, and Nick Nicholson's words about them: "We took her west for more than 100 miles, and over-canvassed her." We decided to go west. If the strategy failed, we would arrive after everybody else. If the strategy succeeded, we might do really well. Everything hung on one factor, namely how soon the wind switched back to the southwest, the prevailing direction in June. I did not share my thoughts with the crew, for they may have thought, half correctly, that I was a pompous ass, but the question crossed my mind: on a first-rate ship of the line, what would Horatio Nelson have done?

Pirate sailed to a point in the ocean that lay 93 NM to the west of the rhumb line,

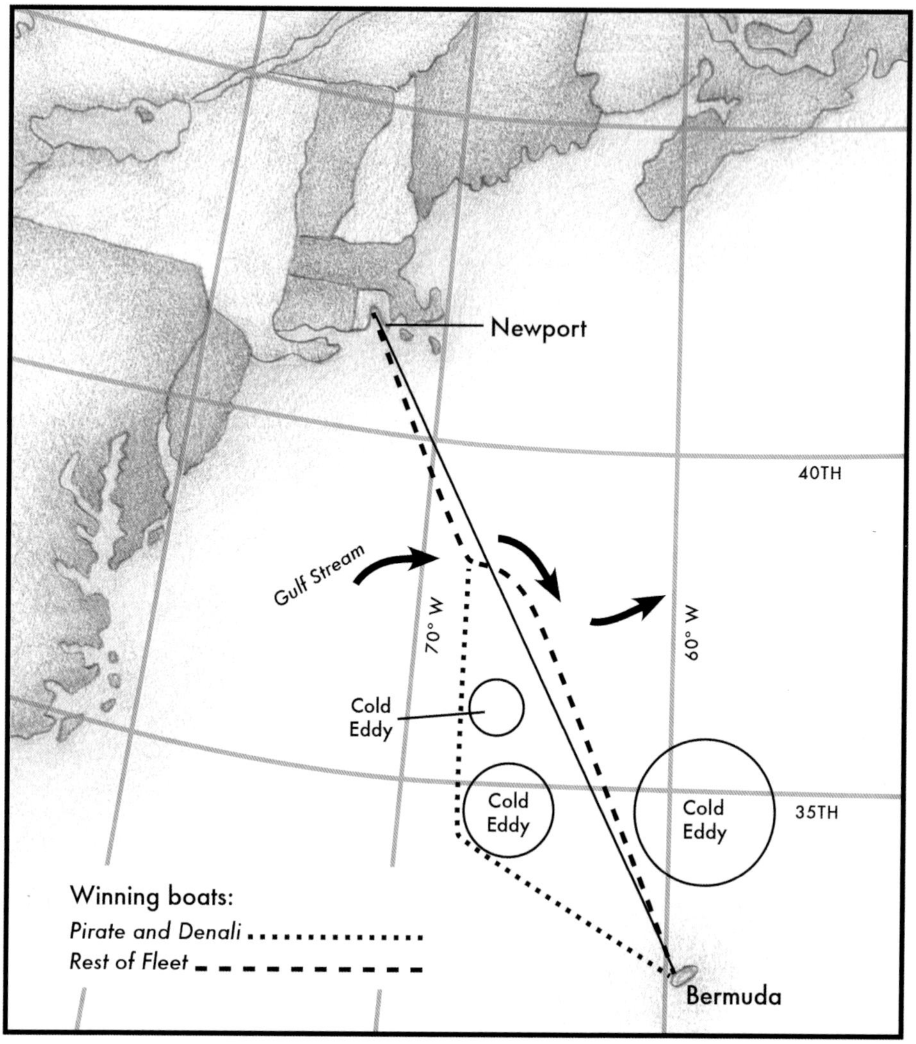

Winning course to Bermuda, 1990

far away from the bulk of the fleet—and from Bermuda. We hoped to pick a certain Gulf Stream meander, then catch a cold eddy or two, and if the wind switched back to the southwest, we would be the first to pick up a roaring reach to Bermuda, with wind on the beam. Sid White, *Pirate*'s navigator, was a veteran of the Gulf Stream, and a reputed wizard with the eddies. But even he turned pale as we sailed many miles away from the other boats. At one point we were sailing some 70 degrees away from Bermuda, to a chancy appointment with the wind, in the blue nether world. Like Columbus, you have to believe in what you are doing, or in your luck, or in divine providence, to keep that up. The crew starts getting nervous, and the first rumblings of mutiny may develop. As on Columbus' ships, even the best mariners, nay, especially the best mariners, feel that their tactical skills are being wasted by the suicidal strategy of the skipper.

The wind shift came on Monday, just as we entered the swirl of a cold eddy that would help us tack back to Bermuda. From there on, it was smooth sailing with none of the thrashing that the boats along the rhumb line got. No more dagger looks from the crew. The grins on their faces started to resemble smiles. Unknown to us then, only one other yacht had chosen the westward strategy too. She was Lawrence Huntington's cat-ketch *Denali,* a yacht created by Jerry Milgram of MIT. He combined the Ron Holland-designed aluminum hull of former British Prime Minister Edward Heath's last *Morning Cloud* with the unconventional rig of his own conception. *Denali* and *Pirate* picked them right—a bit of the meander, the eddies, and the wind shift—and won the Racing and the Cruising Divisions respectively.

The Cruising Division had its most dramatic moment when one of the maxi boats, *War Baby*, had a crewmember swept overboard by a big wave, while attempting to secure a loose reaching strut. A fellow crewmember dove, still attached, and managed to rescue him. On *Pirate* we had one, much safer, melodramatic moment, as a swivel tackle on the jib exploded after midnight. The sail came loose, and the watch went to the foredeck to refasten it. As the search light was turned on and orders were given, an errant flying fish landed inside the shouting mouth of the watch captain, he was baptized Fish-Face Simon.

Meanwhile, *Pirate* had distance on *War Baby* and the fleet. First we rode part of a southeast meander in the Stream. When the effect of the meander started to peter out after 35 miles, we tacked to the west for a risky leg of almost 100 miles. After the wind shifted, the last tack gave us a 300 NM straight reach to Bermuda. Catching two eddies in the right spots at the right time, we reached a speed of 10 knots over the ground.

We got an indication of how well we were doing on Wednesday at noon, our fifth day out. By the rules of the race, the yachts still racing were required to radio their positions to Hamilton. Boat after boat reported that they were north of us, that is, behind us. We started to get excited. We charged across the finish line, shook hands, played Wagner—what else but *The Ride of the Valkyries* on the tape deck, uncorked a bottle of champagne, then made our way through the reef channel to Hamilton, where we tied up. We were ignorant of the final results, but happy we had made it safely, and as fast as conditions allowed. That night at dinner in Hamilton, I cautioned the crew to take the rumored news that we were ahead in our division with a grain of salt, to sleep soundly on real beds, and wait for the next day.

When morning came, we visited the Royal Bermuda Yacht Club. The results were being announced, with boats still out at sea. *Pirate* was leading the Cruising Division. Then came the final announcement: *Pirate* first. We had won five of the big cups. Our navigator, Sid White, was a gentleman of the old school, not outwardly emotional, but there he was sitting on a bench by the yacht club, with the yachts all dressed in the background, my wife and I next to him, when he shouted from the top of his lungs, "How sweet it is!" All that was left for me was to fax the news to friends, call, as promised, to *Pirate*'s previous owner with the news, then take everybody out for dinner. We waited one more day for the bugle to sound at the Governor's mansion, for the presentation of the trophies.

Especially thrilling was *Pirate*'s award as the highest placing boat over 15 years old. That was magnificent, and such a credit to Sparkman & Stephens, and to Olin Stephens in particular. Nick Nicholson, who was present at the awards ceremony, was visibly moved. "Twice in the past, and now this" he said. "Don't you think it has something to do with the boat?" I could not have agreed more: *Pirate* was probably the best specimen of the "all-around" design.

Victory aside, a captain's work is never done. I had to assemble the return crew to take the boat back to Rhode Island. As good seamen know, the return trip from Bermuda is often more hazardous than the racing thrash. Boats are stressed, and the returning crews are often not familiar with them. The weather and the Stream can turn nasty any time and test their stamina. Luckily for us, the return voyage was a

The Pirates take the silver

Skipper Juan Corradi

lovely cruise. The crew was varied and convivial: my wife Christina, our dentist and friend Don, a lawyer and avid sailor named Gennaro, and Mark, a young member of the Bermuda Constabulary, both a seaman and a cop. We all got along royally and sailed the boat efficiently: we beat *Pirate*'s winning time by one hour!

The summer came to a close royally, as grandly as it had begun. Christina and I met my parents in Spain, and in Bayona, overlooking the sea, we met King Juan Carlos, an avid sailor himself. It was the perfect end of our Bermuda fairy tale.

A RECOLLECTION

Winning the Bermuda Race

By Sid White

Chair, Navigator's Committee of the Corinthians

Winning the Bermuda Race is something some of us dream about but never expect to achieve. When it happens—Wow! What a rush of emotion and pure elation! Past Master Bill deNeergaard was watch captain and I was navigator on Pirate*, a Swan 38, which finished first in class and first in the Cruising Division in this year's [1990] Newport to Bermuda Race. I'm not normally outwardly emotional, but sitting in the ambiance of the Royal Bermuda Yacht Club and the colorfully dressed yachts, I shouted as loud as I could "How sweet it is!"*

It's okay to talk about "How you play the game." That's compensation for the losers, but coming in first in the Bermuda Race makes you suddenly realize winning is "everything."

Pirate *is owned and skippered by a professor of sociology at NYU in New York. We also won a cup for the best time in a boat 15 years or older. Our boat was built in Finland 16 years ago.*

This year, for the first time, the traditional Newport–Bermuda Race included a Cruising Division (no spinnakers), and Pirate *was the first to win that honor. There were two classes in the Cruising Division, about 30 boats in all. Interestingly, the cup for the New Division was donated by the Argentine Yacht Club in Buenos Aires, and our skipper is an Argentine. There were 148 finishers in this year's Race. First place in the Racing Division went to* Denali, *a cat-ketch homeported at the Indian Harbor Yacht Club in Greenwich. Although the two divisions were tallied separately,* Pirate*'s corrected finish time placed us second in fleet, right behind* Denali. *Not too shabby.*

The secret of our success was in forecasting a wind shift to the southwest, and moving our boat to take advantage of it. Denali *went 120 miles west of the rhumbline;* Pirate *went 93 miles west. Most of the rest of the fleet sailed right down the rhumb line, and had to tack continuously, spending much of their time going sideways.*

As navigator and tactician aboard Pirate, *I was determined to take advantage of the current and the wind—spurred on by the fact that I had made the race six times previously and the best result had been a fourth in class. Although it was circuitous, I ran the boat hundreds of extra miles to take advantage of the elements. First, we went 35 miles west of the rhumb line to find the top of the Gulf Stream meander, then sailed southeast with the current for more than a hundred miles. When that petered out, we tacked over and went 93 miles west, then tacked again and ran for more than 300 miles on starboard tack right to the lighthouse on Northeast Breakers, on the northern edge of the reef bordering Bermuda. On the way, we went through the south-flowing wheel of the eddy, getting an extra push from that.*

We started getting an indication of how well we were doing on Wednesday at noon, our fifth day out, when we heard radio position reports of boat after boat reporting they were still north of us. After crossing the finish line, we contacted the Royal Bermuda Yacht Club to see how we had done, and were told we were the only boat in our class to have finished at that time giving us first in class, first in the Cruising Division, and second in fleet overall.

* * *

SID WHITE was navigator in seven Bermuda Races and numerous other contests at sea. He was a teacher of celestial navigation, editor of *The Mainsheet*, a publication of The Corinthians, and chairman of the Committee on Navigation of that sailing organization. He worked for Dow Jones and was once a Vietnam War correspondent stationed in Japan.

2

Designed to Perform

Beauty is either the resultant of force vectors
or it is nothing at all.

—Theodor Adorno

It is perfectly possible for machines to be objects of beauty, even of great beauty. Every so often the forces that guide object design proceed unimpeded; technical conditions are ripe; independent lines of evolution converge. Then it happens: a beautiful object is born. Afterwards the heroic aesthetic moment passes. But the object that came into existence under the old stars will keep the glow of its original radiance.

To sail is to move a boat across the water with the wind. But boats differ according to how they provide answers to these questions: how far? how fast? how big? how comfortably? how safely? The history of yachting is a tangle of sinewy trends. One is the lineage of cruising boats. Another is the evolution of racing machines. Converting one type of boat into the other type of boat seldom yields good results. But the classic Swans were an exception (a "classic" is defined in the last chapter of this book).

Boats were often dissimilar, and among those passionate for speed under sail, racing rules were devised to help determine who would win.

It was important to agree on ratings, measurements, and handicaps. As racing rules evolved, designers and builders started working "for the rule." Hulls and sails changed accordingly.

The invention of glass reinforced plastic (GRP) after World War II had an important impact on design. Before, some wooden boatbuilders had experimented with serial production. This was the case of the Herreshoffs of Bristol, Rhode Island, (who inspired Henry Ford) and of Abeking & Rasmussen in Lemwerder, Germany. With fiberglass hulls, boats could be serially and easily produced, based on a mold. Boats changed from artisanal objects to mass-produced things. The evolution of materials continues: from traditional wood to cold-molded construction, from GRP to carbon fiber, and in the not too distant future, to additive manufacturing, or 3D printing.

The world of boating became more complex. Disparity prevailed. Yet for a while the streams seemed to converge. Between the mid-1960s and the mid-1970s, the experts got together to work on a racing rule that could apply worldwide. The International Offshore Rule [IOR] was established in 1970, and had a marked impact on design. The rule fostered international racing of an intense kind. The championships combined short races with an overnight race and a long offshore race. As a result, the boats had to be proficient in both speed and liveability and serve several purposes at once. The combination presupposed a certain type of sailor, numerous in the second half of the 20th century.

In the early 1970s, the builders, the designers, and the rule makers collaborated in the production of boats of great integrity. The firm of Sparkman & Stephens in New York, and Nautor in Finland, best exemplified that rare convergence of factors. Classic Swans evolved as an amalgam of the touring boat and the racing boat. They were hybrids that could be raced, but could also serve to cruise in a relaxed way. With few modifications, they could be taken to the starting line, and when the races were over, they could be sailed home by a family. Later, as yacht racing became more complex and professional, boats were built exclusively for racing purposes, far away from the concerns of normal amateurs. It started with rules like the IOR, and has culminated

Color Drawing of *Pirate*, by Luca Ferron

PIRATE

NEW YORK

with the America's Cup as it progressed. The apotheoses of this type of esoteric yachting are recent editions of the America's Cup races, sailed in multihulls on foils. On the other hand, production boats are designed exclusively for recreation. The classic Swans stand almost alone as stubborn survivors of a bygone golden mean. The S&S Swan 38' sloop named *Pirate* formed part of that exceptional batch of racer-cruisers. (For a full description of the species, see Matteo Salamon, *S&S Swan. A Legend*; Milano and Florence: G&R Association and Viol'Art, 2016.) I had the good luck of stumbling upon a successful member of that species, which we sailed from 1989 until 2010.

According to a legend of the North, swans—which are white—are silent birds that only sing upon approaching death. But if a swan sings, dies, *and* resurrects, then she returns to the water as a black swan and lives forever. *Pirate* was always black.

Who made this particular black swan? To know them one must recall their history as shipwrights and seafarers. In 1630, when Finland and Sweden formed a single nation, shipwrights travelled north from Stockholm to the port of Pietarsaari, called Jakobstad in Swedish, to build ships. Later Finland fell under Russian domination. After a century as a grand duchy under the tsars, the Finns declared independence on December 6, 1917 in the middle of a communist revolution, which prevailed in Russia but was crushed in Finland after a short civil war. The relations between the two countries was always tense. On the eve of World War II, the Soviets demanded land from the Finns as a buffer from the forthcoming Nazi invasion. The Finns refused, and the Russians invaded Finland with a large but inexperienced army. The Finns resisted in the bitter 1939-40 "Winter War" (minus 30°C) in which they managed to bloody the red bear's nose. Finland lost 25,000 men, the Soviet Union lost 240,000.

In the end, the tiny country was forced to cede land in Karelia, and the Finns who lived there resettled in the rest of Finland. Some of them were master boat builders who went to work in Finnish yards. They were the craftsmen who, years later, would build the classic Swans at the Nautor factory in Pietarsaari. This working port, 140 miles south of the Arctic Circle, received several waves of skilled shipwrights from the south and from the east.

In 1966 a young and enterprising boat builder, Pekka Koskenkyla, founded

Nautor in Pietarsaari. He decided to adopt fiberglass, GRP, as the new material for the building of sailboats, and to start production in series. With this—then daring—project in mind, he searched for a designer. He went straight to the top: he approached Sparkman & Stephens in New York, and the Stephens brothers, Olin and Rod, took a chance on him. "Nautor's instructions," said Rod Stephens, "were clear and to the point: to design a top quality product that would be strong and seaworthy."[2] Nautor wished to build a 36 footer, based on *Diana*, a winning One Tonner designed by S&S in 1966. The Swan 36 was launched within a year. In 1968, the Swan 36 *Casse Tete II* demolished the competition at Cowes Week. A legend was born.

The Swans were strong, simple, and fast. Every system was plain, functional, and capable of repair at sea. Nautor and S&S produced other "hits," notably the Swan 65 of 1973. At the time, this was the biggest fiberglass stock sailboat ever built. The Swan 65, *Sayula II,* won the first Whitbread Round the World Yacht Race, crewed by Ramon Carlin, a Mexican businessman and his family; they ate proper meals on china plates while they beat other racing machines staffed by experienced pros. *Sayula II* epitomized the ideal of the all-around yacht and the perfect charter boat.

The Swan 38 was one of the six Swans designed by Sparkman & Stephens after the Swan 65. The 38 project dates back to 1973, with the first boats delivered in 1974. The original drawing (Design No. 2160) was a One Ton effort from S&S. The prototype hull, named *America Jane II*, was built of aluminium at the Royal Huisman in the Netherlands. It was a result of extensive tank tests at the Davidson Laboratory in New Jersey. Rather long and narrow for a One Ton, *America Jane II* did not display the radical beam of some other designs, although the short keel and full afterbody were in keeping with the norms of that era. The cockpit was both large and high, with the helmsman seated aft and the winch crew working forward. The shortened cockpit seats provided access to a sail storage for heavy sails, while the Volvo diesel was located under the cockpit floor. A steep companionway ladder led to a bare cabin, with berths on both sides near the main hatch. A simple galley was to port, and the chart table to starboard. A curtain pulled across forward of the keel-stepped mast to provide privacy

[2] Cited in *Swan 25 Years. A Boat International Publication*; Surrey: Ward House, 1991; p.6. For a full account, read Pekka Koskenkyla, "How the Swans Were Born," in *S&S Swan. A Legend*, p.13-31.

for the head. The entire bow area was devoted to light sail storage. The yacht carried only six gallons of both water and fuel, and a small alternator provided electricity for the electronic equipment. *America Jane II* was a pure racer.

The Swan 38 was based on this prototype, but with more amenities to suit a racer-cruiser. The result was S&S design No. 2167: a boat with an aggressive air but also the purity of line that caught the eye of an aesthete. Olin Stephens managed to draw pleasing lines unaffected by the necessary concessions to rating and volume: the true touch of a *maestro*.

In the prototype, the deck was flush except for a small cabin blister that extended from cockpit to just forward of the mast. When Nautor produced the design, the coach roof was streamlined and became an extension of the cockpit coamings. This feature (first tried on a Swan 48 in 1971) became the hallmark of several generations of Swans. Image matched performance. The surfaces flowed into each other. The Swan 38 had graceful overhangs, a straight sheerline, a discreet reverse transom, and a sharp stem. The hull was beamy yet balanced like a champagne glass, without excessive freeboard.

The first Swan 38 left the yard in Pietarsaari on 4 April 1974, and as many as 38 Swan 38s were delivered between April and December of that year. By the 70s, Nautor had an assembly line that could have been the envy of Detroit in those days. Out of all the models that Nautor produced since 1966, the Swan 38 was the most successful, if judged by sheer numbers: 116 yachts were built between 1974 and 1978. The model was designed to rate as a One Tonner with a short rig. At Sparkman & Stephens, William G. Mavrogiannis was in charge of the project. The boat had fine ends and was deep in the water. The fine veed entry promised efficiency to windward. On a smaller scale, it resembled the famed Swan 65. The Swan 38 and the 65 became mythical boats, mixing performance and beauty, as did some of the Herreshoff sloops, or the Concordia yawls, in previous eras.

Olin Stephens' design made this possible: a moderate displacement hull, low in the water, with ballast stability and additional form stability, with weight collected at the center. These factors allowed a very generous sail area and made the vessel strong, safe, and fast in any seaway.

Hull 019 was sold in 1974 to Alan McIlhenny by the Nautor office for the United States and Canada, then headquartered in Maryland. He baptized her *Pirate*, and she kept that name (with a short exception).

The boat was built in the tall rig version, with 2.5 extra feet of mast, and so carried more canvas than the One Ton model. In this version the boat performed admirably on almost every point of sail. As the boat gathered many miles and many stories, she came into her own—a good performer on most points of sails, competitive in long-distance ocean races.

The teak deck was ordered on April 10, rather late for the yard's schedule. The bottom of the boat was not treated with antifouling paint until her arrival in Boston, and no gas bottle was supplied due to the different system of propane in the US. At Nautor, the standards of quality and completion were such that the owner was given a yacht ready for service. Lars Ström, who knew then and knows today all classic Swan yachts inside and out, carefully supervised the technical details. His recollections and technical notes appear in *S&S Swan. A Legend.* Among Swan owners, Mr. Ström is known as "the professor."

Nautor assured skilled workmanship. As the boat was built, all chips, shavings and other foreign matter were removed, and all parts cleaned before the application of paint. When delivered, the boat's bilges and pockets were close to sterile. All compartments were accessible for cleaning and painting. The same was true of the engine, steering gear, and all other equipment that required service. Rod Stephens closely supervised the rigging. His notes and correspondence detailed all proportions and specified the provision of sails. The scantlings and materials were consistent with what in 1974 was considered a light hull, though stiff and strong. It was built of glass fiber reinforced polyester by the hand laying-up method with the approval of Lloyd's Register of Shipping. The structural bulkheads were built of marine-grade plywood, laminated to hull and deck. The stiffeners were fiberglass lay-ups over foam cores. Web floors were also made of GRP laminated to the hull. The engine seatings were made of GRP with steel inserts. The ballast keel was a lead casting with antimony. The cast-in bolts were made of stainless steel. The lower flange of the mast step took the keelbolt nuts. A docking shoe of stainless steel was fitted to the lower edge of the keel. Finally, a single point-lifting lug was fastened to the keelbolts. The entire structure spoke to confidence at sea. The rig anchorage added to that feeling. The mast was carried through the deck. The mast bulkhead was reinforced with GRP to take the stainless steel chainplates. A bracket laminated inside the transom supported the backstay chainplate. The whole thing was terribly strong. After 20-odd years of hard sailing, only the rudder shaft showed signs of hardening. A fax to Nautor produced in return a complete set of the original plans, and notes on how specifically Hull 019 was built. I had the shaft replaced with a new one made with carbon fiber.

The steering gear used steel cable, and had sheaves with guards to prevent jamming. The aluminium steering quadrant was bolted to the rudder shaft, and was easily accessible for inspection and lubrication. It worked faultlessly for at least 37 years. The factory installed a pedestal with a sprocket and a friction brake. The compass went on top. The boat also carried an emergency tiller, easily connected to the shaft. An elegant detail was the integral spinnaker pole tray, or "gutter," one on each side of the coach deck. The woodwork on deck was all teak. A hundred other details are typical of Swans of the mid-seventies. After years of sailing, some of these fixtures corroded, and the teak decks needed replacement. Their lifespan is 20 years. A refit every decade or so has kept the black Swan as fresh and spry as when she was first launched.

Pirate's deck fittings signified "Nautor" to anyone familiar with yachts: the anodized toe rail with one pair of hawse holes amidships, and lugs for spinnaker sheet blocks at extreme quarters; 12" mooring cleats, two on the foredeck with fairleads, and two aft to the toe rail, and a powerful stem fitting of stainless steel, with bow roller and double foresail tack attachment. With a full crew and an afterguard, this small boat could be raced anywhere, but she was also kind to a cruising couple, not hell-bent for speed. She could sail along a familiar coast or cross an ocean to unknown shores. The boat could pass severe offshore tests. Some books carried the drawings of the Swan 38 as the standard reference for bluewater cruising and racing.

The interior was spartan and cozy at the same time: an icebox, foot pumps for water, and powerful manual pumps to clear the bilges. The joinerwork was superb. Teak was used in all visible woodwork. The floorboards were finished with laid teak veneer, and provided easy access to the bilge. The interior topsides were lined with teak. Tables, bureaus, seats, and dressers had rounded corners. Doors, partitions, and panelling were plywood. The door sills had stainless steel chafing pieces. Hanging lockers had rods, and their doors were provided with louvers for ventilation. Drawers had to be lifted to open. The companionway ladder was not too steep. Except for the pipe berths forward, all berths were equipped with canvas leeboards and 4" thick mattresses of flexible foam. Every detail was practical and thoughtful. The fore cabin had sail bins under the folding pipe berths. The main cabin had a drop-leaf table with fiddles, with stowage for bottles and glasses in the foot. The aft cabin had a double berth to starboard and a single berth to port. The navigating space had a good table, with room for instrument displays and a chart drawer under the top. The galley and the navigator's seat were equipped with safety belts to enable the navigator and the cook to work in safety. Over the years, the instruments were upgraded, as sailing moved from the sextant era to that of GPS, radar, and chartplotters. The head was simple and functional: mirror, sink, a hand shower, and the classic Baby Blake. The galley was bare but efficient, with a propane stove and oven. The boat's machinery was kept simple. When the boat sailed towards northern Norway, she was equipped with a diesel heater and a duct that turned the head into a drying room. In her lifetime, *Pirate* had several diesel engines, from a 20HP Bukh to a modern Beta 28. The controls in the cockpit were simple. There were five seacocks throughout the hull, all made of bronze and easily serviced. All tanks were of welded stainless steel.

The ventilation of the boat was appropriate for Scandinavia, but a little less effective in warm climes. The electrical system had strong wiring and was accessible in all parts. The interior lighting was almost perfect.

The mast was massive, with a strong elliptical section. The wiring was internal. It had a stainless steel spinnaker pole track, two eyes on each side for the jockey pole, and a main halyard winch on a welded base. The main boom was of round section with a worm screw outhaul. The standing rigging was stainless steel 1x19 wire with Norseman terminals. The backstay adjuster was a rigging screw with handles. The headstay had toggles at the upper and the lower ends. Finally, the boat came with mooring lines, and carried two anchors with chain and rode. The gear could be as simple or as extensive as the need arose, for racing, coastal cruising, or offshore passages.

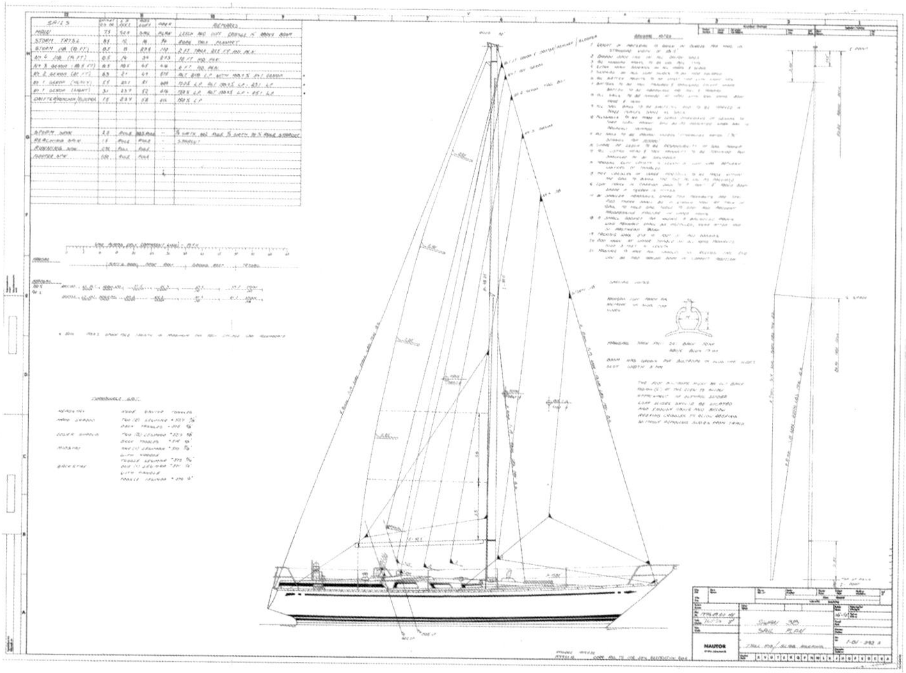

Drawing from Sparkman & Stephens, from *Swan–A Legend*, Matteo Salamon, editor. By permission.

Equipped with the original gear, *Pirate* left the factory by truck on June 16 1974, and was shipped from Helsinki to Boston the following day, together with her sister-ship *Gaylark*. (As of this writing, the former *Gaylark* is still racing in the Mediterranean as one of Vicente Onorato's *Mascalzone Latino* yachts.)

In the fall of 1973, McIlhenny had sold his Morgan 33, and wanted a new boat. He saw an ad for the new Swan 38, and the description fit his needs. Dr. Kaighn Smith, an old friend and future commodore of the CCA, had the same idea. The two men ordered boats on the same day. They were the first two Swan 38s to reach North America. They arrived in Boston on the same ship on July 1st, 1974.

The boats were unloaded at the container port in Charlestown. After a few days of repairs and preparations, *Pirate* was ready for her first sail, with none other than Rod Stephens on board.

Rod Stephens prepared a report on *Pirate*'s shakedown sail. He noted that the soft engine mounts allowed excessive motion when the engine was being started or stopped. He also suggested minor corrections on the boom for slab reefing. But he was pleased: "*Pirate* was beautifully prepared for trials and with the exception of the details mentioned, the hull and rig were absolutely best quality."

In her first summer *Pirate* sailed to Northeast Harbor, Maine, her first home port in America. The yacht participated in the Portland–Monhegan Island Race. Then she sailed to Annapolis, where she participated in the Maryland Fall Series. In a letter to Rod Stephens, Mark Ewing of Nautor's Maryland office commented on the early performance of the boat (letter supplied by Mitch Gibbons-Neff):

> *The day before the race, Bob Angell persuaded Alan McIlhenny, the owner of* Pirate, *the second of the 38's we have sailing in this country, to race. Due to the impromptu nature of their decision to race, they ended up with the owner and his wife, one of our secretaries in the office here, Bob Angell and his wife, and two young kids that work at the yard. In other words, four girls and four guys none of whom had sailed together before. In any event, they ended up finishing fifth in their class of twenty-five or twenty-seven boats in what was approximately a two-third moderate to fresh beat and in the remaining distance, a close reach and a run.*

Pirate wintered in the water at Oxford, Maryland, and was made available for inspection as a model for potential customers.

In 1976, *Pirate* sailed from Maine to Rhode Island in order to join the fleet for her first Newport–Bermuda Race. It turned out to be a very slow race, and *Pirate*'s performance was not stellar. They abandoned the race and motored 30 hours in flat sea conditions to reach Bermuda. Then the skipper and friends sailed the boat from Bermuda to Northeast Harbor directly. That summer *Pirate* raced again in the Portland–Monhegan Island Race, and she was hauled out for the winter in Maine.

Pirate's racing record was a disappointment to her first owner. Her sistership, *Gaylark*, with a different keel and rudder configuration, had more success. See McIlhenny's explanation in his letter, following. He writes that in her early days, *Pirate* reached a top speed of about 10.5 knots. A few years later, surfing under storm conditions, *Pirate* managed to reach a dangerous 13 knots!

In 1977, McIlhenny sailed *Pirate* locally in Maine, and decided to sell her. The yacht was shown to potential buyers in Northeast Harbor. In the winter of 1978 Max Mehlburger, an attorney from Little Rock, Arkansas, bought the yacht and started a new chapter in the boat's life.

A RECOLLECTION

The First Years

A letter from Alan McIlhenny, First Owner and Skipper

In the fall of 1973, having sold my Morgan 33 the previous summer, I was casually interested in a new boat when my eye caught an ad for the new Swan 38. I was immediately certain that that was what I wanted.

Kaighn Smith, an old sailing adversary of mine (and friend) had the same idea. We ordered boats on the same day. These were the first two Swan 38s to reach North America, arriving as deck cargo on the same container ship in June of 1974.

The name Pirate *comes from my notion, when I bought the Morgan 33, that Morgan was a famous pirate, and my boat would be* Pirate, *a famous Morgan. I was pleased enough with the name to keep it for the Swan, though I am not sure the resulting black color is great in the tropics.*

Dr. Smith's boat, Gaylark, *is named for his three children: Gay, Laurie, and Kaighn (pronounced Kane).*

The two arrivals were off-loaded at the Boston container port (Charlestown) on the Mystic River. I first boarded Pirate *on the deck of the container ship, just after they tied up. Things were in some disarray. There seems to have been a break-in when the ship stopped in Hamburg, though nothing appeared to be missing. There was some weather damage from the torn canvas cover and an open hatch.*

There followed a delay while customs people worried about who had been in the boat before inspection. Because of union rules and high labor costs, the containers had to come off first. Then, when the trucks and containers were all gone, the boats were deposited on land, papers signed, and finally, after the ship departed, we hooked up again to the huge terminal crane and were lifted out over the water and dropped into Boston's Mystic River.

My son, Alan, Jr., and a friend of his, James Murdock, were with me. The trick was to start the engine right away and hope everything was all right. Once we unhooked, we were on our own in the tidal currents. There were no boatyard craft to help us. Our mast was in two pieces, lashed to the deck. It was either motor or drift in the steamer channel.

Gaylark *followed us in. Bob Angell, from Nautor, was aboard with his wife. We led the way to Manchester, beyond Marblehead, about 20 miles. Both boats were hauled there, shipping scars were patched, bottoms painted, IOR measurements taken, and boats launched and rigged. All this took about four days.*

The head of the yard, Jack Brengle, was an old friend of mine. I had taken him on a cruise in 1939 to St. John, New Brunswick, where we had sailed my chartered 40 footer over the reversing falls and 60 miles up the St. John River.

Our sails came over from Hood in Marblehead the evening before our first sail. The mainsail was wrong! Back it went to have the slides replaced with slugs. There was considerable urgency as Rod Stephens had announced he was coming up from New York for the first sail the next morning.

It was Rod's custom to go on the first sail of each new design, to make sure it was right. First thing on the boat, he asked to be hauled to the top of the mast. The Hood loft manager, also along, was put to work cranking him up. Stephens bossed him around all day like he was a cabin boy.

Rod brought along a small vial of pure lanolin from a drug store. He put the oil on all sheave and shackle pins and turnbuckle threads. This he did from the bosun's chair while inspecting everything aloft. He also marked the main halyard wire to show the maximum permissible hoist.

Back on deck, his next move was to remove the compensating magnets from the compass, no permission asked, and throw them overboard, saying they caused more errors from misuse or casual meddling than they prevented. Swing the compass he said, and use a deviation card.

After this burst of activity he calmed down and we went for a nice sail in moderate to fresh winds. He left the oil with me and told me to use it regularly. I don't think I ever did.

1974 summary: Sailed to Northeast Harbor, Maine, our homeport. Portland–Monhegan Island Race. Sailed to Annapolis, Maryland. Sailed in Fall Series. Wintered, in water at Oxford, Maryland (then Nautor headquarters, USA), boat available for inspection.

1975 summary: Annapolis–Newport Race. Marblehead–Halifax Race. My son and I two-handed the boat from Halifax to Northeast Harbor. Hauled out for winter in Northeast Harbor.

1976 summary: Sailed Northeast Harbor to Newport. Raced in Newport–Bermuda Race. A very slow race, we abandoned and motored 30 hours in near flat conditions to reach Bermuda. My son and friends sailed the boat from Bermuda to Northeast Harbor. Demonstrated the boat to potential buyers.

1978 summary: Sold the boat in the winter to Max Mehlburger.

Our racing record was poor, a source of disappointment to me. I thought we were better than that. I had won my first sailboat race in 1930 at age ten, cruised extensively, raced at the national championship level, and navigated four Newport–Bermuda Races and two Newport–Annapolis Races in big boats in the 1950 to 1960 decade.

Beating to windward is Pirate*'s weakest point of sailing. This is primarily due to a poor keel design, too thick, too little lateral plane area. Our mainsail was no help either, not enough draft and a leech that sagged off.*

Dr. Smith has a new keel on Gaylark *now and a new spade rudder, which, believe it or not, he installed himself, from Sparkman & Stephens designs. As his special skill was downwind sailing, and his North spinnakers were excellent, he had considerable success from the beginning. This contrasts with my special skill, which was upwind sailing, and which proved inadequate to cope with* Pirate*'s less than sparkling performance in that area.*

I assume all your primary sails are new [1993], but I wonder about that old 2 oz. Dacron spinnaker you refer to in your article on the Columbus Transatlantic Race. That sounds like one of our original Hood sails [it was–JC], designed to be carried as a reacher with the pole on the headstay. I won a local race with that sail when the breeze freshened from abeam after a long 20-mile reach and run. We set the heavy reacher for the last two miles and carried it well. Dr. Smith stuck with his tri-radial and wiped out a few times, letting us break free for a win. Incidentally, we also beat a well-sailed Hinckley Competition 41 and a Hinckley 48 boat-for-boat.

The boat was never what I would call aground. On one occasion we touched a sand bar doing seven knots leaving the mouth of the Choptank, in the Chesapeake Bay, just enough to dip the bow about an inch or two. The boat never slowed down. We also had to leave an exposed cove in the middle of the night when a sea started rolling in at low tide. I felt a touch of firm mud when in the trough of a wave. We left the mooring and motored out without further incident.

Our maximum speed was about 10.5 knots. We were sailing three-handed with the big spinnaker up on a direct passage from Northeast Harbor to the Cape Cod Canal. It breezed on from astern. A following sea built up and we found ourselves surfing down the waves. We decided to get the sail down before dark, which we succeeded in doing, without getting it wet, by winching the clew down to the deck with an auxiliary line.

My wife and I have cruised on Gaylark *with Dr. Smith on several occasions. Recently, in Maine, we had a long beat against a fresh southwesterly. He demonstrated his technique for easy sailing under those conditions by taking down the main and using the heavy #1 genoa alone. The boat sailed fast and balanced well.*

Two years ago he had to leave the boat a day early and asked us to return it from Oxford to Annapolis. We had an exciting sail, finding ourselves running up the Chesapeake in 35 knots under main alone, doing about 11 knots on the speedo, and the youngest of two crew aboard was 70 years old.

* * *

ALAN MCILHENNY (1920-2016) was born in Philadelphia. At the age of 10, Alan became an accomplished sailor. By his mid-teens, Alan and friends were sailing up and down the Maine coast, away for weeks at a time. After Pearl Harbor, he finished his degree early in order to enlist in January, 1942. He was accepted as a celestial navigator with Pan American Air Ferries, a unit that became part of the Army Air Force. He flew 100 missions overseas during the war. In mid-life, Alan became interested in the computer modeling of sailboat racing. He was entrusted by the Cruising Club of America, and later the IMS committee of U.S. Sailing, to develop an 'implied wind system' to enable boats of different shapes and sizes to compete fairly against one another, and to know their handicap during the actual race, not after it. Alan was the 1998 recipient of the Cruising Club of America's Nye Award. (From CCA, *Final Voyages*, 2016)

3

Treasure Hunt

Serendipity is when you realize
that the thing you got
is way better than the one you wanted.

—Pedro Cuperman

My friend Pedro Cuperman, a romantic philosopher and literary theorist, (died on July 12, 2016) insisted on it: I had to have a boat. He had purchased a classic Swan 44 named *Sarabande* and was delighted with it. I wanted something reliable, where I could live if I wanted, and sail wide and long—a vessel that could teach me the ropes. I had not been seriously on a sailboat since my teenage years on the River Plate. While driving along the shores of Long Island, I came upon a stubby Dutch sloop, a Contest 29, built in the 60s. I bought that yacht on impulse, with a real-estate partner. I needed both the impulse and the company, or I would not have bought anything at all.

The summer was intense. I purchased the little boat late in the season, and she needed work. I was traveling a lot: Newfoundland in August, and then Argentina for a full four months. It seemed best to do the work slowly and launch her the following year. The yard loved the plan since, as I would find out later, it was more diligent in sending bills than in doing the commissioned work. Then my partner failed to pay his share, so I assumed full ownership of the boat.

Despite all this, 1985 was a very good year. I made investments in Canada, France, and the US, most of them smart. I was reunited with my family in Argentina after a decade of political turmoil. I published a book. And I had a boat! In spite of superstition, in homage to my birthplace and to a haunting tango, I changed the sloop's name from *Windlass* to *Sur*.

My first experience in boat ownership was awkward. It was comprised of ignorance, fear, and high bills. The bills I paid. Doing more—and worrying less—took care of the fear: start the engine, hoist the sail, drop the lines, hold the tiller, go. Ignorance took longer to correct. But *Sur* imposed herself in strong and beneficial ways. The little yacht repelled all toxic acquaintances and attracted good ones. She made me happy, taught me a lot, and instilled in me a passion for the deep. I was able to fully embrace that passion a few years later, on another boat.

Four summers passed, as I kept learning the ways of the sea, mostly by myself aboard *Sur* on Long Island. Then something special happened to me in the South Fork in the late summer of 1988. Picture this: sunlight, in long angles through the trees in late afternoon—at a small marina at Three Mile Harbor—the docks white and clean, next to the green of the manicured lawn in the marina. Not far from the docks, in the channel, the white of a sailboat, with the wind behind her, sails billowed like wings of a giant bird, going out to sea. *Nos agimur tumidis velis.*[3] On the boat, I am attentive to the sails, listening only to the wind and the surf. A woman and a man are at the dock, waving arms, trying to catch my attention on the sailboat. They are Annika and Manos, Greek friends on a visit to Long Island.

In that world of watery stillness, and a soft breeze, the two at the dock and the man on the boat, received a full glimpse of the future. I had the vision of crossing the ocean in a small sailboat. After that, the world was no longer still. Because of the support of those two friends, Annika Barbarigos and Manos Vernicos, the vision brought sudden opportunity. Henceforth, everything was done to advance a project, seemingly crazy for an academic and a latecomer to the sport: to cross the Atlantic Ocean.

[3] In 1865, the New York Yacht Club was incorporated, adopting the Latin motto: "*Nos agimur tumidis velis*"—"We go with swelling sails" (adapted in reverse from the Roman poet Horace, "Non *agimur tumidis* uelis"—"We do not go with swelling sails", in Epistles, 2, 2, 201).

Sur, my sailboat on the channel at Three Mile Harbor, was too small for a reasonable crossing of the ocean. Though sturdy, and built for the North Sea, she was barely 30 feet long. She was 20 years old, and had not been designed for the high seas. But she had become the object of care, by me, and by my friends as well, who now dreamt of bigger feats. Our vision of a passage called for a different vessel. If and when I found that vessel, her acquisition should in no way be a betrayal of little *Sur*. The small sloop would pass to someone who could care for her and would, in return, give him succor in an hour of trial. She would help him just as she had helped me.

Sur had tolerated my early feats of nautical incompetence. One unforgettable afternoon, my friend, Bro Uttal, and I took *Sur* for a sail near Gardiner's Island. In the course of a few hours, we managed to compress such a wide array of navigational errors, botched maneuvers, and foolish acts as a mariner might commit over the course of a lifetime. The sheer number of mistakes must have imbued us with a sense of destiny. Then, without knowing why, I started making comments on deck in what was a strong and unmistakable Punjab accent. I knew nothing about India but the accent seemed to capture the comic sense of our appalling seamanship, probably under the influence of Peter Sellers in the film *The Party*. Thus the folklore of "Indian Navigation" was born among sailing friends. From that moment, we spun yarn after yarn of Indian Navigation: a ragtag composition of stories from Sinbad, Odysseus, Popeye, and Chief Inspector Clouseau. The yarns were edited, added upon, and compiled. Diplomas of Indian Navigation were issued to those deserving them, and Indian Navigation became an ineffable style and common bond in our small band of sailors. That happened before the dour squall of political correctness descended upon our merry world.

The years went by. The original Indian Navigators learned a lot more, but the lore survived, and amazingly, was confirmed by events in the real world. Reality imitates art. In the spring of 1989, the Nautor Swan newsletter *Underway* featured a story about a special round-the-world voyage on a Swan:

> *Many Swans have sailed the world, but perhaps none in such fashion as* Trishna. *Owned by the Indian Army and sailed by a team of soldiers in January 1987, she touched the Gateway of India after a 15 month, 30,000 mile passage around the world. Not only was* Trishna *the first Indian yacht to complete such a*

voyage, she surely must be the only Swan 37 to have done so.

After an initial delivery trip from England, where Trishna *was purchased, to India, she sailed from Bombay in September '85 straight into cyclonic gales until Mauritius. Then rounding the Cape of Good Hope for St. Helena, the Cape lived up to its second name, the Cape of Storms, as the wind touched 65 knots and the waves broke between 40 and 50 feet. The ensuing Caribbean seemed tranquil in comparison, despite seven days of 30 knots between Barbados and Jamaica.*

Passing through the Panama Canal, the crew then made good time covering the 3,200 miles from the Galapagos to the Marquesas Islands non-stop in 21 days. Then on to Tahiti and further storms to Rarotonga. Fiji gave a pleasant respite, but 50-knot winds blighted the fetch to Auckland with sails torn and hand-repaired. The worst was to come; in the Tasman Sea from Auckland to Sydney, the August timing proved unfortunate as the southern wind dished up a five-day storm with 60-knot winds and 40-foot seas crashing across the boat. The same storm caused serious damage on the streets of Sydney.

Resting in Sydney, the team set out for Brisbane, then on to Cairns and Thursday Island with its navigational hazards. Trishna *grounded on one of the many unmarked reefs but was freed without serious damage. The sail down to Darwin lightened hearts, as did the leg back to Asia, first port of call being Kupang in Timor. Then, with perhaps some of the finest sailing of the trip, came Bali, Jakarta, Singapore, Penang, Colombo, and finally the Gateway of India in Bombay on January 10th 1987.*

Nothing we had invented compared to this tale, yet in our own way we were as determined to cross oceans as *Trishna*'s soldiers. One day we too would sail about the world on a Swan that would forgive our mistakes.

The same year that I started on *Sur*, 1985, was an extraordinary year for the Swan 38 named *Pirate*. In June, she scored a magnificent victory in the race from Marion to Bermuda, described earlier. Her owner and skipper, Max Mehlburger, chose a high-risk strategy by sailing the boat hundreds of miles away from the fleet, to the west of the rhumb line, in search of a wind shift, and a fast point of sail. When the expected change of wind occurred, he tacked the boat towards Bermuda, as if hitting the precise

A RECOLLECTION

The 1985 Marion to Bermuda Race

Charlie Bascom interviewed Max Mehlburger, skipper of *Pirate*, a Swan 38 that won overall in 1985. Mehlburger hailed from Little Rock, Arkansas. Bascom asked him how he knew he'd done well approaching the finish line in that race.

"The first indication that we'd maybe done well was when we heard Herb Marcus [Silkie], *a Tartan 41 in Class C, make the VHF call to the Finish Line Committee. I remember thinking that we must be doing pretty good if we were that close to Herb...*

Pirate *was ninth across the finish, just after 7 am. The wind was howling, so we pulled into St. George's and rafted up beside a Swan 48, with none other than William Hurd on board. Hurd delivered this soliloquy to his own shipmates. "Now look at this little 38-footer. These guys did it right—this is the way you're supposed to do it..."*

You see, most boats stayed close to the rhumb, whereas we were rather radical. My navigator, Nick Nicholson, and I listened carefully to the weather forecasts, talked it over, and—I know this sounds crazy—we went 110 miles west of the rhumb line. The wind shift was about 24 hours behind schedule and we were wringing our hands, but finally it veered and there we were, windward of the fleet. The poor guys on the rhumb had it right on the nose. Then the wind came up. We were on a beam reach and we all took turns seeing who could make the boat go fastest. There were times when Pirate *was surfing at 14 or more, down the face of the waves, all day long. That's really how the race was won."*

—Mark Gabrielson, *Corinthian Resolve*, 2017, p. 110.

spot on a band in a billiard shot. She led a fleet of 150 boats and placed first overall on corrected time. Yet more was in store that year.

Mehlburger decided to leave *Pirate* in Bermuda rather than return her to a pleasant summer sailing in Newport. His plan was to sail the boat to Antigua after the hurricane season in the fall. He elected to depart in November, as soon as the tradewinds arrived. To head south in the trades at that time of the year was a prudent choice.

Pirate and her crew could look forward to a delightful sail of about six days covering a distance of approximately 900 miles with a landfall on Barbuda and then Antigua. In Mehlburger's words, they anticipated "sliding effortlessly along to large but gentle swells created by the full fetch of the Atlantic from Africa in winds 15 to 25 knots with bright sunshine, perfect temperatures, and dry decks." (from "*Pirate*'s Log—Bermuda to Tortola—1985," by Max Mehlburger, *Mainsheet*, Little Rock, Arkansas; January 1, 1986.)

In November, Mehlburger sailed from Newport to Bermuda with three friends aboard *Beachcomber*, a new Hinckley 59 that they helped deliver for her owners from the Midwest. In Bermuda, *Beachcomber*'s owners and the rest of *Pirate*'s crew boarded their boats for expected "idyllic" trips south, to St. John and Antigua respectively. The two crews moved their vessels from Hamilton to St. George, spent time together sampling Gosling's rum, and completed their provisioning. On November 12, just after lunch, *Pirate* set sail for Antigua.

The weather forecast in Bermuda predicted perfect tradewind conditions. There had been two late season hurricanes in 1985. The second one, named *Juan*, occurred when such storms are all but unknown. In those years, the hurricane season usually extended from July through September, with occasional storms in June and October. One third of all hurricanes recorded have taken place in September, which is therefore considered the most dangerous month. A third late season hurricane in the middle of November was most unlikely, so Mehlburger and his crew left Bermuda in high spirits. *Pirate* had every prospect for a swift and happy passage.

The logbook entries for the first two days confirmed the optimistic expectations. The weather was clear; the winds, about 20 knots true; the seas 4 to 8 feet. *Pirate* close reached at just under 7 knots under single-reefed main and a #3 jib, on course for Barbuda. On their second day at sea, the crew had a pleasant dinner, tasted German wine, and listened to a selection of songs that Kaki Hockersmith, Max Mehlburger's wife, had given him for his birthday. The entry for the next day at 1400 hours showed that *Pirate* had sailed 318 miles right on course. The skipper and the crew dutifully checked the weather two or three times each day by SSB receiver. The forecasts continued to be good. The barometer, which was at 1043 mb when they left

Bermuda, dropped very slowly and steadily to 1034. The drop was not alarming. On Friday, November 15, the deduced reckoning position had the vessel slightly east of the rhumb line, 460 miles from Barbuda.

The weather changed however. Clouds appeared. The wind increased. At noon that day *Pirate* encountered a short squall with winds about 48 knots true. The boat ran off in the squall under double-reefed main, without a jib. After the squall, *Pirate* proceeded along her course, under a double-reefed main only. She then encountered a second squall with winds around 50 knots. But this "squall" refused to pass. (See Sidebar, The Hurricane.)

The weather forecasts now mentioned somebody named *Kate*. A tropical depression developed, then rapidly compressed, and formed a hurricane. *Pirate*'s position, about 120 miles north northeast of the eye, was on the dangerous semi-circle of the storm. The crew felt the wind speed climb to more than 60 knots. *Pirate* was clearly in major trouble, on the bad side of a surprise hurricane, with winds that reached Force 11 on the Beaufort scale! To complete the picture, the crew soon saw what they had only read about before in Adlard Coles classic book, *Heavy Weather Sailing* (New York: John De Graff Inc.,): "waves of 35 to 40 feet are not uncommon in an average hurricane and, in giant storms, build up to 45 to 50 feet."

Thanks to good leadership and good seamanship, and also thanks to her noble features, *Pirate* went through the serious storm in great form and survived it with grace.

After the ordeal, *Pirate*'s crew sewed up the main by hand in the cockpit (the only damage they found was that the seams were over-stretched), and got sunburnt under blazing skies. Later in the day, they had to bear some nasty thunderstorms and strong gusts, perhaps the parting salvos of the storm. *Pirate* altered course: Mehlburger and his crew decided to make for nearby Tortola, giving a wide berth to the treacherous Anegada reef. They learned that *Beachcomber* had also weathered the storm. That boat hove to and waited out the hurricane, without injuries. However, the hatches on the Hinckley leaked like waterfalls, whereas all the bunks on *Pirate* were completely dry. Others were not so lucky. A 42' sloop named *Taxi Dancer* was dismasted in her attempt to follow *Pirate*'s same strategy. The crew was taken off and the yacht was taken in tow by a ship. Unfortunately, another boat in the area had sunk out from under its crew. The emergency radio signal from their life raft alerted an airplane crew who radioed the Coast Guard. The ship was directed to rescue the life raft crew; and the skipper of *Taxi Dancer* gallantly agreed to scuttle (sink) her to expedite the rescue of the life raft crew. The crews of both yachts were safe, but both boats were lost.

"In retrospect," Melhburger wrote, "I am very proud of *Pirate* and the crew. We came through a serious storm with no injury and relatively insignificant damage. We all feel that the experience, while not one we wished to have or would want to repeat, was a very valuable one. We learned a lot about ourselves and our reactions to stress and fear. Our confidence in *Pirate* was amply justified and strengthened. We will go to sea more safely next time because of the experience. Finally, we will go to great lengths in the future to avoid hurricanes!"

* * *

After that visionary afternoon in Three Mile Harbor, a partnership was formed between the skipper of *Sur* and the friends who had waved at her from the dock. It was a generous sponsorship, as Annika and Manos shared with me the dream and the expenses, but not the voyage itself.

Annika and Manos lived in Greece aboard the yacht *Freedom* but travelled to New York and New England often. Their 60-foot motorsailer was built in 1920 as a cruising yacht for the English lakes. The yacht had moved from England to Greece and was restored in a yard at Perama, near Athens. *Freedom* was much more than a showpiece: the ship bravely sailed where few others of her kind dared to sail. In 1987, I learned her ways in a gale, which I shared with my friends. That hard and beautiful sail cemented a comradeship in arms between Annika, Manos, and myself. The search for the right boat was on. It took Manos and me to the shores of Lake Michigan, to inspect a sistership of *Trishna*, a Swan 37 named *Dulcinea*. But she was not quite right, and the price too high. The search went on.

Back in New York a year later, Manos introduced me to the firm of Sparkman & Stephens, and the S&S family introduced us to *Pirate*. The name first appeared in the brokerage list provided by Mitch Gibbons-Neff and Rex Herbert of S&S. Later on I

The 60 foot "Freedom" under way off the Greek coast. Built in 1920 at White's yard in England, she has been lovingly restored by her latest owner.

Motorsailer *Freedom*, built in 1920 for the English lakes

would also meet Alan Gilbert, then the chief engineer of S&S, who became my friend. The boat was not among their favorites. So it was in a casual mood and without any great expectations that my wife-to-be, Christina, her mother, Julia, and I drove one chilly morning in February of 1989 to the yard where the boat was kept.

She had been in a yard for over a year. The workers at the Jamestown Boatyard were so fond of the yacht that they started a joint effort to purchase her. Their effort did not prosper but ours did. It was a bit of a wild place. A winding dirt road in the island of Conanicut, past Jamestown, led us to the ragged edge of the water. We passed a private boathouse and some big summer houses, then closed after the season. We reached the entrance to the yard. Two sheds, a pier, a shingled office, and a strong smell of seaweed greeted us. Near the shore we saw the sharp profiles of the Dumplings, a series of granite rocks that studded the entrance to the mooring field. Across the bay lay Newport, the mecca of American yachting. Behind the sheds was an area no larger than a parking lot, full of boats on poppets, some covered, some exposed. The wind was biting cold and whistled through the spars. It took some time to find the boat. But then my eyes caught the razor edge of her bow, different from the surrounding hulls.

I placed a ladder on the topsides, climbed aboard and looked from the deck out to Narragansett Bay. *Pirate*'s bow pointed to the sea, as if she wanted to go. Christina climbed up as well. We found the keys to unlock the companionway, and went below. Inside she looked like a miniature Scandinavian furniture shop with designs from Alvar Aalto, but streamlined for heavy seas. Rounded lines and edges showed that the Finnish carpenters knew their craft. The lockers looked good. The boat was well-equipped. The main problems were the decks, which looked tired, and the bottom, which suggested that perhaps osmosis might have attacked the hull underwater. We sat in the cockpit and looked at each other. If there were no serious structural problems, and the price was right, this was indeed the boat. The rest would come in due course. The sail inventory, on paper, was luxurious: 21 bags of sails.

The Swan 38 was known in sailing circles and beyond. It had inspired a book, in 1978, a thriller that was riveting and taut. It was a story of revenge in the high seas, in which a doctor, cruising on his yacht across the North Atlantic is run over by a giant tanker. The man survives, but his wife and the boat are lost. The hero is determined to get even and to chase, like Ahab, the big monster to destroy it. Instead of a harpoon he will use a rocket. He looks for a new yacht: she must be a swift sloop, small (to sail her singlehanded) yet strong and fast. There is only one logical choice and the author, Justin Scott, after considerable research picked the Nautor Swan 38. My overall purpose was different however: to pursue happiness, not the big whale. The doctor found his Swan on a mooring, and we found ours in a yard, but the thrill of the encounter was the same. Here are Scott's words on the classic Swan 38:

> *A fresh wind raised a chop on the water and snapped the yachts' halyards musically against their aluminum masts. These were deepwater cruising and racing boats. They droned past a spectacular white hull, a Sparkman and Stephens Nautor Swan built in Finland. Hardin gazed longingly at her powerful lines. It would be*

hard to imagine a finer singlehanded cruising boat. They were rare in the States, but he had once seen one in Boston. The view stopped swinging and then Culling slowed the little engine, Hardin turned around and saw the Nautor Swan, twenty yards ahead. Even moored it looked like a prowling shark.

'That,' said Culling.

The Swan had the short, sharp lines of a bayonet, powerful rather than pretty, with its bow not especially raked and its squarish stern chopped at a distinct forward angle. A sliver of cabin wedged barely a foot above the deck at its highest point.

Hardin turned from the straight lines of the hull to Culling's sly face. 'What are you up to? She's got to cost more than I have.'

She was beamier than her sharp profile suggested, and Hardin paused for a heady moment at the aluminum helm to drink in her wide teak decks and lavish fittings and imagine what a joy it would be to work her. This was an ocean yacht capable of driving as hard and far as a man could push.

—From Justin Scott, *The Shipkiller*; New York: The Dial Press, 1978, pp.41-44.

For us, the following months were hectic. The survey was positive. I purchased the boat at a reduced price, but the hard part lay ahead. *Pirate* underwent a complete overhaul. The general strategy was simple: no frills, but no false savings either. To that end, *Pirate* was in the right place. Though small, with touches of a family operation, the Jamestown Boatyard had an experienced management, and it was a Swan service yard. Over the years, the yard had developed a working knowledge of the Swan systems and construction, moving from troubleshooting minor problems to major overhaul and deck replacement jobs. The yard sent crew members to Finland for technical training. Fax machines (no e-mail at the time) were kept busy passing questions and specifications between Rhode Island and the Finnish factory. The yard could track the history of each vessel and perform preventive maintenance.

The Jamestown crew started with the hull. They sandblasted and ground the bottom of the boat, dried it thoroughly, and applied an epoxy barrier coat. They ground, glassed, and faired the rudder. Only then did they apply bottom paint. They next faired the topsides. A black hull has special problems. When painting the topsides with a high-gloss paint, the fiberglass roving will show through after a few years. This happens because the heat from the dark hull continues to cure and shrinks the paint. The workers took care of this in the careful fairing of the topsides. We remembered Captain Nathanael Herreshoff's words: "There are two colors for a boat: white and black—and only a fool will paint her black." But we kept her dark and shiny as befits the eternal swan of Finnish legend. We found stress cracks but they were on the surface of the fiberglass. They were repaired. Next came some carpentry on the decks. The mechanical systems were thoroughly overhauled: we changed filters and siphon breaks, and strainers too; we installed a new muffler, a new cutlass bearing, and added a three-blade feathering prop. We installed a new engine, a 29 HP Perkins Perama. The electrical wiring was changed. The bonding system was cleaned. As for the rigging, we left nothing untouched: backstay and headstay, shrouds, turnbuckles. We put a new mainsheet traveler, built a new boom, freed up all the sheaves, lubricated all 13 winches, replaced lifelines, and softened everything that was stiff. The job was well-executed, and the price tag matched the quality. For the first two seasons, *Pirate*'s main instrument of navigation was the checkbook. *Pirate*'s refit was featured in *Practical Sailor*, Vol. 15, No.15-16, August 1989, p.23. She regained her former splendid looks, and had offshore races to run and oceans to cross, and many miles to go.

Had it not been for one of the early Clinton imbroglios, *Pirate* and I would not have met. In 1978, when Bill Clinton was attorney general of Arkansas, he and his wife, Hillary, partnered with James and Susan McDougal to purchase 220 acres of land that would become the Whitewater Development Corporation. The real estate venture failed, costing the Clintons a reported $40,000 in losses. James McDougal subsequently entered the banking industry, forming Madison Guaranty Savings and Loan. In 1986, federal regulators investigated another real estate investment backed by James McDougal. The investigation led to McDougal's resignation from Madison Guaranty and the eventual collapse of the bank. One of the investors in these deals was a friend of the Clintons, a lawyer and brilliant sailor from Little Rock who owned

Aquisition and refit In 1990. (Photo credit: *Practical Sailor)*

and campaigned *Pirate* for a decade. He lost his money and had to put the yacht up for sale in 1988. I knew nothing of that when I started looking for a boat.

Friends in Narragansett Bay involved with getting *Pirate* ready for her future exploits, are some of the finest sailors I know: Bill Biewenga, Aaron Jasper, Nick Nicholson, Chuck Poindexter, Phil Steggall, to name a few. Those were happy days.

A RECOLLECTION

The Hurricane

by Max Mehlburger, "*Pirate*'s Log: Bermuda to Tortola–1985," Part II
Mainsheet, Little Rock, Arkansas, February 1, 1986.

On Saturday, November 16, the radio broadcast from Portsmouth, Virginia, informed us that the tropical depression mentioned for the first time only a few hours before had become a hurricane named Kate. The position of the storm's center was given as 21.5 North, 65.0 West. Our DR (deduced reckoning) position at that time was 23.5 North, 63.5 West. Which placed Pirate 128 miles and 038 degrees from Kate's center. Winds we estimated at 60 knots were from the east and seas were exceeding twenty feet. We could only estimate the strength of the wind since the digital readouts at the navigator's station and on deck had quit working. The analog instruments were still working fine; however, the analog anemometer only reads to 50 knots where the needle was 'pegged.' The northeast quadrant of the storm had strong winds out 300 miles from the center; and the southeast quadrant had strong winds extending some 50 miles from the center. The hurricane was stationary and had not moved from the location where she had formed. If she had moved from somewhere else to that point, we would have had a better idea of where she might move next. More importantly, we would have had an earlier warning of the presence of the storm and could have perhaps sailed easterly while our wind was from the southeast and not so (damn) strong.

At this point we decided to furl all sail and stream warps from the stern to slow the boat as much as possible. The idea was to stay relatively stationary and let the storm move away from us. We dragged a 200' anchor rode in a long loop astern of the boat with each end led through a fairlead and secured to a winch. We attached a loop of chain around the rode and threw it overboard to keep the rode below the surface. Then we attached two large, strong buckets to two spinnaker sheets and dropped them overboard. The boat's speed was thus reduced to about 3 knots. We stood our watches through the night, steering to keep her steady on her heading. Several large waves broke aboard during the night, filling the cockpit with water and stimulating the deck watch, but doing no actual damage.

On Saturday morning, the situation had deteriorated significantly. While the wind was still from the east, it had increased somewhat to 60–70 knots. The height of waves is a function of wind strength, fetch (distance over open water), and time. Since the wind had been from the east for 20 hours, the seas were becoming impressive, perhaps 30 feet trough to crest. Our warping strategy was not working because the storm center was not moving, meaning that we were gaining on the storm! If the situation continued unchanged long enough, we would slowly revolve around the eye like a cork in a whirlpool. We had three options: (1) we could continue warping and hope the storm would move away from us; (2) we could set sail and close reach out on starboard to the northeast; and (3) we could try port tack to the southeast. The problem with warping was that we had no assurance the storm would begin to move any time soon. Strong winds extended from our position approximately 175 miles to the northeast and 100 miles to the southeast, making port tack look more attractive. Two other factors influenced the decision. While we were on what would normally be the 'dangerous' semicircle, as long as the storm was stationary there was no difference between semicircles; therefore, port tack across the dangerous side was a viable option. Also, the delights of Antigua beckoned to us from the southeast!

We decided to make sail and proceed on port tack. We took in the warps, which was no small trick since they had become one gigantic hawser, twisted perfectly as if by a rope-making machine. Since different lines were led through the close fairleads at the stern, they could not be simply winched aboard. One bucket, having survived the night, now stubbornly resisted our efforts; the other was gone. We could have cut everything away, but what if we needed to warp her again? By bending a strong line on the 'hawser' and leading it to a halyard winch near the mast, we were able to retrieve some of the warp. By continuing this process, the warps were finally gotten aboard. We then set the #5 jib and the triple-reefed main.

I had been apprehensive at times during the storm, but when I prepared to turn the boat upwind into the huge waves I was truly terrified by the thought of letting the boat get caught wallowing helplessly in a trough under a big breaking wave. As it turned out, my fears were largely imagined. The boat responded instantly, charging willingly up the face of the oncoming wave I had more or less selected for the moment of truth. I was overcautious for a while, barely keeping enough speed to climb each wave as it came at us; but as things went along I began to realize that the strategy was very reasonable. There was no fear of pitch poling (stern over bow à la catamaran), which typically occurs when a boat is running down a big breaking wave. We were meeting the waves with great power and speed and wonderful maneuverability. We still had to worry about being rolled; however, I discovered that I could usually pick the place to go over each wave to avoid a breaking area by staying on the backside of the previous wave a little longer or by diving down into the trough at a sharper angle. As my confidence in the concept grew, it became exhilarating. We were making 10 to 12 knots close reaching into large seas under good control, heading away from the storm and toward Antigua! At 1145 hours a weather report gave us the good news that the storm had begun to move westerly at 5 knots, the best possible direction for us. We were further cheered by the thought that Kate was on a direct course for the presidential palace in Havana! We continued in this way from about 1000 hours until 1730 hours, covering 70 miles.

As night approached, we knew we could not continue our magnificent end run; going that fast in the dark would have been suicidal. We furled the main just in time, for a number of seams along the leech had opened. The sail had done an incredible job for us, making the strategy possible. We proceeded along the same course with only the #5 jib at much reduced speed. An hour after dark an astonishing thing happened. In one minute or less, the wind suddenly dropped from 70 to 25 knots! It seemed like a flat calm. The seas were still mountainous, but they quickly lost their viciousness. We slatted around under-canvassed all night with only the #5, superstitiously hesitant to make more sail; however, the strong winds did not return and Sunday dawned cool and sunny. The morning weather broadcast informed us that Kate had moved further away to the west during the night. We had come through the hurricane with no injuries and only very minor damage to the boat.

* * *

MAX C. MEHLBURGER is an avid sailor and a lawyer who served Little Rock in Real Property Law, Domestic Relations Law, and Commercial Litigation cases. Max and his wife Kaki were friends of Bill and Hillary Clinton. For eight years, decorator Kaki Hockersmith worked closely with the nation's first family to create a home in the White House that reflected its personality. When I visited the Mehlburgers in their Italianate villa in Little Rock, I was shown a room dedicated to *Pirate* memorabilia, a veritable shrine to the boat.

4

Into the Great Western Ocean

I only know one way of finding out how far one can go,
And that is by setting out and getting there.

—Henri Bergson

In the city of Paris, *passage* refers to the arcades: covered streets connecting boulevards, and offering sometimes mysterious and enticing merchandise. The poet Louis Aragon called them "human aquariums: .... places that were incomprehensible yesterday, and that tomorrow will never know." I feel like that about ocean sailing, where a crossing from the mainland to a distant isle, or between two continents, is called a *passage*.

To cross an ocean on a small sailboat is part of a unique and ephemeral cult. It would be incomprehensible to the mariners of yesterday, who sailed for necessity, not sport, and it will be probably unknown to the humans that will follow us. Amateur ocean sailors may be a doomed but enchanted breed, as the ageing and shrinking membership of their organizations (the venerable Corinthians is a case in point) testify. I am proud to belong to them, and wish to leave this modest record of our damnable pleasure.

It started like this. On a bright day in late April of 1991, I composed a note to *Pirate*'s volunteer crew for our passage, containing a schedule for launching, sea trials, provisioning, routing, departure date, watches, and miscellaneous details. I sent the memo to two men working in offices in New York, and to my wife Christina, who was part of the crew. It was a "state of the boat" report, and a wish list. Yet things happened pretty close to schedule and according to the plan, with few exceptions (one experienced sailor dropped out and a young Harvard undergraduate replaced him). There were just four of us and a big ocean to cross: Simon Wynn from Australia, Hanno Schloendorff from Germany, Christina Spellman from New York City, and myself, an Argentinian in America. The note comprised six precise categories, with a list of things to do, but there was no Number 7, telling them to remember to write a will.

The days before our scheduled departure, I lived on *Pirate*, making her ready, and waiting out a vicious nor'easter in Rhode Island. On June 6, the wind veered and the weather turned pleasant. The weather reports from meteorologist Bob Rice gave us the green light. The rest of the crew arrived the day before departure. All provisions were stowed, all tanks topped, the dinghy tucked away, and we all went to sleep waiting for the next day.

At 0815, after breakfast, we cast off from Jamestown. The barometer was high, the sky clear, and the wind blew in the morning at eight knots from the north. We left under power, getting ready to hoist sail at the sight of Brenton Reef. But the stuffing box was too tight, and it overheated. Despite efforts to loosen the nut, it remained too tight. It seemed silly to continue with the problem when we were still so close to shore. So we returned for repairs. Instead of tying her to the dock, we put the boat directly on the rails to lift her up. Once out of the water, I replaced the anode around the shaft, while the workers at the yard solved the stuffing box problem. And there was time enough for two members of the crew to drive to nearby Newport to retrieve a forgotten nylon drifter that would prove useful in the light summer airs of the Mediterranian. By four in the afternoon everything was fixed, the boat was re-launched, and we started again.

Narragansett Bay faded in the haze. There I was, the least probable of seamen only a few years before, facing the great blue, minding the vessel with family and friends. Christina, Simon, and Hanno were confident enough, or crazy enough, to trust *Pirate* and me with their lives. It was a drastic way to leave the city and its chores for an adventure both simpler and more demanding, closer to nature, to life and death. The academic in me bemoaned the sorry state of my discipline, sociology, which I once joined in the hope of making the world a better place. The thinker in me bemoaned the death of spirit at the university, transformed from a place of high learning and idle curiosity into an information vending machine with a stable of celebrities as part of the publicity brochure. But the sailor in me was not at all sorry for those disappointments, or for the killjoy life that had replaced them. Before me stood the prospect of raw survival at sea.

At 1700 hours, we cleared Brenton Reef again. The afternoon breeze blew from the southwest, at 16 knots, and fell to half that by nightfall. Calm rollers rocked the boat. The sunset was bright orange; a trawler passed astern. We set our wind vane, baptized "Alfredo", and it performed flawlessly, as we moved at five knots. Night fell gently upon us, as *Pirate* braved the first majestic ocean swells. We practiced star sights and started our watches after the first dinner under sail. The moon rose before midnight, and at 0300 we changed course further to the east. We entered another world, where an ever-present horizon had replaced the future.

Dawn greeted us with Homeric rosy fingers, cirrus clouds, and seven knots of breeze, on a very broad reach. It was time to fly the spinnaker. Shortly after noon we cleared Nantucket Light, and the ocean came alive with creatures: marauding sharks to port, three lazy pilot whales to starboard, and playful dolphins all around the boat. We doused the spinnaker late in the afternoon, prepared for another night, took star sights at 2100 hours, and encountered some haze, then fog, which made us nervous, given the proximity of the shipping lanes. Cold arrived too, and the cries of unseen birds sounded infernal at times. Alfredo continued to steer, while one of us remained on watch at all times.

The following day the sun burnt through the fog. As soon as the apparent wind crossed the threshold of 12 knots, *Pirate* lurched forward under full canvas, and reached a speed of seven knots. She was telling us: "Give me wind and I shall give you miles." We sighted more whales at noon. We were now 200 miles from shore. We chatted over the radio with a Lyons Lines cargo vessel, and a little later with a container ship bound for the Azores, like us. We flew the kite again under ideal weather conditions. To our delight, we discovered that the autopilot could steer under spinnaker!

On the third day of the voyage we started monitoring the sea temperature, because it would tell us when we entered the Gulf Stream, or the "Blue God." Since we were approaching the current from the west, where its "wall" is sharpest, a sudden jump in temperature would be a sure indicator that we were at the mercy of the Blue God. From NOAA charts and their surface temperature analyses we had an approximate idea of the coordinates of the Gulf Stream, its eddies and meanders. We were about to enter the largest river on earth—which is in the ocean—some 300 NM east of Rhode Island.

In the wee hours of June 9 the moon rose. The sea temperature jumped from 20°C (68°F) to 26°C. By 0430 it reached 30°C (86°F). We were fully inside the Gulf Stream. Our instruments (in those days both Loran-C and an early GPS) put us at 38°46'N, 065°03'W. The tremendous force of the current was in our favor, supplementing the southwest breeze that blew at 14 knots. Together, wind and stream gave us a speed over the ground of just below 12 knots.

But the Blue God is finicky. It is a magnet for odd forms of marine life (Portuguese men–of–war, sargasso weed, lazy turtles, flapping sunfish, basking sharks, regular sharks, flying fish, phosphorescence), and for squalls. The skies were first hazy, and then cloudy, with signs of the first squall approaching. *Pirate* kept cutting the waves at a steady clip on a pleasant beam reach. In the afternoon, squalls and whales arrived, at the same time. We put a reef on the mainsail. A large thunderstorm loomed on the horizon, then dissipated. In between squalls, excited, happy to be underway, I called my family in Argentina on the SSB radio, and reported our position and the state of the sea. We continued under reefed main and #3 genoa, a combination that suits a Swan 38 well for breezes over 20 knots on her beam. The squalls left us by midnight. The skies cleared; the barometer rose, the wind dropped a bit. The new breeze was weak and on the nose, so we lost speed. Things improved in the afternoon, when wind direction and speed made it possible to fly the spinnaker again. But that day (June 10) held a surprise. At 1630, while we ran under spinnaker, ominous black clouds appeared astern. Then, no more than three miles away, a bizarre spectacle unfolded before our eyes: six waterspouts marched, like booted legs of doom, towards us! Human reactions are often contradictory: while two of us thought only of dousing the kite quickly, the youngest member of the crew grabbed his camera as if afraid, not of the approaching twisters, but of missing the photo op! Christina emerged from the galley just in time to see the twisters, but had to go back as the whistle of a pressure-cooker sounded its own alarm. Luckily, the spouts moved sideways and left us in peace, or rather, with just a vulgar thunderstorm.

The weather and the sea calmed down during the night; the pressure-cooker did not explode. The skies became clear, the night balmy. I held the wheel relaxed, enjoying the soft breeze, and then, exactly at midnight, came the last surprise: the pale green folds of a rare, immense sky curtain—Aurora Borealis, the Northern Lights, not common in those latitudes.

The new moon rose on June 11, at 0300, garnished by small clouds. At dawn we got a fix with the sextant, and checked our position with a passing freighter, the Norwegian ship *Pasquale*. Thus started our sixth day at sea, which also brought a radio conversation with meteorologist Bob Rice, very keen on knowing more about our encounter with waterspouts. He advised us to come down one degree in latitude to avoid icebergs. That was our last communication with him, because the SSB radio was disabled by a hidden leak behind the radio. From then on, any communication would be patched through VHF from passing ships. In the afternoon we gybed the kite and talked to another passing ship, *Eolian Star*, carrying cement to New Jersey. We doused the spinnaker at sunset and prepared for another night of squalls in the Gulf Stream. By day's end, *Pirate* had given us 800 miles. On the eighth day at sea we felt cold again, which meant we had moved north of the Stream, away from its main current. We changed our clocks, as we passed through our first time zone.

As per the advice received earlier, we came down to a more prudent latitude (38°38'N). *Pirate*'s speed steadied at six and a half knots over the water. On the ninth day we changed course due east. Dolphins came to play. We were resigned to radio silence: we were truly alone in the middle of nowhere.

The night brought stronger winds. They built steadily to Force 7, and the waves reached ten feet. A gale was brewing, taking its time, as Atlantic gales do, to ripen and reach full strength. It never became severe, just a near gale, but the rough seas made the crew queasy, and the skipper fully seasick, though able to stand watch and steer in a grumpy mood. The system lasted 36 hours—standard for an Atlantic blow. We set a second forestay, and hanked on a strong #4 jib. With such a small heavy jib and two reefs in the mainsail, *Pirate* moved in stable ways, without noticeable loss of speed. The wind vane relieved us from manual steering. The watch huddled under the dodger, tethered to pad-eyes on each side of the companionway. Twice did breaking waves hit the deck like an explosion, but without damage. The cockpit was flooded twice, but drained itself in little time. A Swan 38 inspires confidence in any seas, and every time the small cockpit got pooped but returned to normal on short notice, I thanked Olin and Rod Stephens, and the Finns for having produced such a good vessel. The companionway was closed except during the change in watches. *Pirate* kept moving at six and a half knots—a confident boat, eating the miles.

When the gale subsided we had covered 1,300 NM. The wind backed, and the seas were finally calm. On the 11th day we set the spinnaker again, and sighted an inquisitive whale to port; clearly a humpback. We made noise by dipping a second spinnaker pole in the water and banging it with a mallet, to drive the beast away. We were not ready for Moby Dick.

The next morning the wind freshened a bit from the southeast, and *Pirate* accelerated again, as we breached the magic 12-knot barrier of apparent wind speed. Again dolphins surrounded the boat, determined to gambol and leap. When playing music below decks, the vibrations made them jump and snort, as if dancing with the waves, and I am convinced they prefer Mozart to jazz. We changed the ship's clock again: 1,500 miles under the keel, and another time zone went by.

June 18, our 13th day at sea, was uneventful. The wind abated and moved to the southwest, allowing us to sail on a broad reach, with staysail and jenny first, and then under spinnaker. A hint of island life: a Bermuda Longtail hovered overhead. We were approaching the island of Flores. We established our position at 38°42'N, 031°26'W by celestial navigation. We located Flores with the Radio Direction Finder, a receiver for finding the bearing to a radio source. When the GPS came back to life (it was a slow early version of the Magellan that we were learning to use) it confirmed our celestial fix. On June 19, we sighted the ship *Rainbow Hope* and established VHF contact.

The communications officer kindly placed a phone call to the US for us, and told our families that we were alive and well, and approaching land.

June 20, our official 14th day at sea, started with the excitement—and apprehension—of an imminent landfall. The skies were covered. The air was hazy. We sighted lights at 0200. An hour later we saw a commercial vessel far astern. But then, as the fog lifted, in front of us, massive and grey, the isle of Faial and the volcano of Pico became visible. Another sailboat, from France, was coming in as well. On the radio, they said they were veterans of the landfall, and invited us to follow them into the harbor. We doused the sails and revved the engine, and something strange happened: after two weeks at sea, we were moved almost to tears at the sight of land. Landfall after a first ocean crossing is a strong, unforgettable experience. At 0625 we docked by the office of the Portuguese port authorities, and I set foot on land, holding boat documents under my arm. My sea legs made the land seem wobbly. My emotion made me feel I was walking on clouds.

We had done it in record time: 13 days and 11 hours after leaving Brenton Reef we were in a land of rolling hills, small houses, well-tended gardens, new accents and different faces. Soon enough we would visit Peter Azevedo's famed *Café Sport*, haven for mariners, communications center, and the hub of gossip in the middle of the Atlantic Ocean. But before venturing into civilization, we took the precaution of procuring good showers, with hot water and soap! We had averaged 138 miles a day, with our best daily run estimated at 160 miles.

What about sustenance? It was surprisingly simple and healthy. In our experience on *Pirate*, we never had problems with food or provisions. When we first started going offshore, *Pirate* had no refrigeration, so we had to provision for long periods at sea without sacrificing the pleasures of good cuisine. Carrying enough water was crucial. The first few days were easy: flash frozen meats and other fresh foods that take a few days to thaw, could be stacked in the ice box, and after they had been consumed, we moved to dry goods. Ever since the first crossing, we used this type of provisioning as the default mode, even after installing refrigeration and a watermaker on board. A simple fourfold table determines what you will need. All you have to do is cross two binary variables: Refrigeration (+/-) and closeness to land (+/-). The rest follows.

A Recollection

Provisioning *Pirate*

By Christina Spellman

As we contemplated a transatlantic crossing, the question became how do we provision for 30 days on a boat where there would be four people and no refrigeration? Pirate *had a large and well-insulated ice box and we had a great Italian stove with an oven plus sufficient storage space. The challenge was to have good nutrition, tasty meals, avoid monotony, and to enjoy the meals we had as much as possible.*

As with coastal and weekend cruising, dry goods staples like crackers, rice, pasta, tinned tuna fish and tomatoes were easy. For this trip we set ourselves the task of learning to be pre-modern. Our idea was to scour mediaeval and ancient recipes that would be used in winter before the advent of mechanical refrigeration.

Bread after the first few days would be a challenge, however, we had two easy solutions: German long-life pumpernickels and a recipe for beer bread. The beer bread, which turns out to be similar to English muffins (or at least it did for us), had an unexpected advantage: baking cleared the humidity out of the cabin. Plus, the smell of baked goods was a morale boost.

Citrus was essential since we all knew the history of scurvy and the British Navy's discoveries of its therapeutic powers.

Proteins were a challenge. A clever butcher found a 10-day answer; he agreed to flash freeze meats layered in the order of how likely they would be to spoil and in the size of an ice block that would fit in the ice box. The chicken was eaten first and by the time we reached the lamb nine days later, it could be marinated in red wine and herbs for two days—by which time we only had a few more days to the Azores. An equally clever friend procured a whole prosciutto, which lived in the fore-peak, and made it all the way to Sicily. The secret was to cut any moldy piece off, and then wash the fresh piece with vinegar.

Lunch and alternate meals sometimes used bacalao, dried cod made with a variety of recipes involving potatoes, onions, olives, garlic—variety being the secret to enjoying repeated use. Here we were channeling the Nordics and the French recipes for this versatile (depending on what accompanies it) food. We also channeled dairy farmers and carried many hard cheeses, such as parmesan, and cheddar, which were tasty and long lived. Toasted prosciutto and cheese sandwiches were a staple.

One secret we learned was to take unrefrigerated eggs with us, in cartons that could be rotated each day. Rotation kept them from going bad. We also experimented with sprouting beans, concocting cassoulet-like stews, curries and generally deciding that the culinary adventure was a part of the sailing adventure.

Another secret was to use the wind vane at dinner time, despite the rigorous watch system, so that the four of us could share a meal.

In the first transatlantic, we arrived in Horta, hungry for fresh foods and eager to touch land. We were all in good health, never felt starved, and seldom were bored with our meals. Morale was high, as was camaraderie.

The first painting on the seawall in Horta.

Horta lived up to my best expectations about ports of call. The green fields, the hedges of blue hydrangeas, the peak of neighboring Pico, the pink-stucco homes, the old-fashioned stores, even the long lines at the bakery (good for getting local gossip in addition to bread), the clean public baths, the laundry service, the room we took at the Pousada da Horta (in the Fort of Santa Cruz), the inimitable *Café Sport* (we had café au lait and toasted sandwiches two hours after landfall), made us happy. Over the bar at Peter Azevedo's establishment, I spotted a message for us, a telegram from a German friend, with good wishes, and calling us *arditi navigatori*.

These were days before easy communication, when sailing was global but still romantic. It required perseverance, patience, and pause. We made phone calls, made purchases, and made two paintings on the long sea wall, marking our arrival. We washed our oilskins, and I climbed the mast to check the rig. We bought supplies, sampled the wine, tasted *chourizo*, and the classic *bacalhao*. Portuguese food is not for feeble stomachs: full of flavor and spice. Wary of catching port fever—talk, talk, and never sail, is a common disease in Horta—we decided to leave town in two days, and use the time to take a look at another island. We chose Graciosa.

When we first arrived in Graciosa we tied to the dock in the old town of Santa Cruz, but the surge made it untenable, so we set off again in search of an anchorage or a better dock. This we found in the village of Praia. Desolate and melancholy, it reminded me of an outport in Newfoundland. The little houses, the small church, the wooden planks to dry the fish, and the little square covered with garlic heads drying in the sun, spoke of simple lives, the fear of God, and respect for the sea. A huddle of children surveyed the boat and us. It was a safe place to leave the boat and tour the island in an old Mercedes, driven by a nice man who offered his services for the day at a reasonable price. We visited a sleeping volcano, with meadows on the rim of the crater, and Wagnerian caves full of bats and sulfur lakes.

The next day we sailed away and set course for Point St. Vincent, on the mainland of Portugal. We divided the leg into five separate waypoints, correcting course to keep due east. Our destination was Vilamoura, near Faro, in the region of the Algarve. The only important trick was to stay far enough to the north to make use of the prevailing winds. On that leg, it is easy to correct course to the south, but almost impossible to beat back north. The Portuguese discoverers had done it, Columbus had done it, Drake had done, Nelson had done it, and so would we. We did not want to end up in Gibraltar prematurely, before our various appointments in Portugal.

We left with a good wind, 29 knots on a broad reach. But the wind moderated to a steady seven knots, and we set the spinnaker, confident in holding that sail through the night. But in the middle of the night, the wind increased and the spinnaker blew out. We managed to retrieve it from under the boat with only a small tear, and we gybed on to a different course. Then the wind died; we were becalmed for the next three days, right in the middle of the Azores High, typical of those latitudes at that time of year. We waited, tried to fish, took a dip or two into the salty ocean, and then motored for almost a day, trying to escape the doldrums.

During that calm we came to understand how polluted the ocean is: we saw garbage, oil slicks, even furniture floating here and there. Christina kept the crew in good spirits through culinary feats. The rest of us played with the sextant, getting a fix by crossing lines of position from the Moon and Vega, a navigational star. The fix put us within five miles of our GPS position. Since the wind did not oblige, we found other forms of useful distraction, such as topping the fuel tank from a jerry can, and making small repairs here and there in the boat. We got used to our slow pace. The days and nights were glorious, and besides, we were in no rush. On the fifth day after we left Graciosa we had covered only 364 NM. The wind teased us: it would increase to what promised to be a sailing breeze, and then slouch back to almost nothing. We sighted more garbage, but also some marine life. A pair of humpback whales on each side of the ship started splashing their tails in what seemed like a courtship dance—not a good place to be, so we motored away quickly.

During this becalmed part of the passage we sighted many big ships. When hailed, few deigned to answer. We soon realized that they were more likely to respond to a female voice than to a male voice, so we asked Christina to act as a modern-day Tokyo Rose. It worked. The lure of the sirens still haunts mariners today.

We tried old mariner tricks to call the wind. Since we could not stick a knife in the metal mast, we whistled, and were answered—but a little too much. As Longfellow wrote in *Complete Poetical Works*; 1893. Christus: A Mystery, Part II. The Golden legend. V. VI. At Sea.

Once a little while ago
I was whistling to Antonio
For a capful of wind to fill our sail
And instead of a breeze he sent a gale.

The wind finally came back with a bang. We lurched forward, under reefed genoa jib and main. Despite my apprehension about freak waves, the boat performed admirably and the wind vane steered us through the confused seas. The wind continued to increase, and as night fell, to a full-grown gale. The glass dropped from 1033 to 1025 mb. We were cold and wet. A big wave broke on deck, but *Pirate* took it in stride. The scariest moment was at 2200 when we sighted a large ship very close to us. We were able to raise her on the VHF, but the captain could not spot us on his radar. We gave him our exact position, course and speed, and turned on the strobe light at the top of the mast, and flew a radar-reflector flag on the backstay, a relic of Operation Desert Storm; American tanks used such flags, with metal strips inside, to keep track of each other in sandstorms. He saw us, and changed course. Finally, at midnight we caught a glimpse of the light on Cape St. Vincent, and an hour later, also the Sagres light, near the castle of Prince Henry the Navigator. We got in the lee of the Cape, and the seas calmed down, even though the wind did not. By mid-morning the skies were clear, the gale turned into a fresh breeze, and we could see the coastline.

We had arrived in the old world! When we docked at the marina in Vilamoura, in the south of Portugal, we had logged 2,981 miles since we left the shores of Rhode Island. Our first Transatlantic Passage was over. And we remembered the saying about "it ain't over till the fat lady sings" when we took a bus to Lisbon the following day; in the old section of town, we heard some formidable ladies—all portly, and some hirsute—sing long weepy *fados*, sad tales of absence in the deep.

O salty sea, so much of whose salt
Is Portugal's tears! All the mothers
Who had to weep for us to cross you!
All the sons who prayed in vain!
All the brides-to-be who never
Married for you to be ours, O sea!

Was it worth doing?
Everything's worth doing
If the soul of the doer isn't small.
Whoever would go beyond the Cape
Must go beyond sorrow.
God placed danger and the abyss in the sea,
But he also made it heaven's mirror.

—Fernando Pessoa

5

In Search of Ancient Worlds

Καθόμαστε γύρω από τη Μεσόγειο,
όπως βατράχια γύρω από μια λίμνη.

We sit around the Mediterranean,
like frogs around a pond.

—Socrates

La Méditerranée est une mer épuisante.
The Mediterranean is a most fatiguing sea.

—Bernard Moitessier

Sid White, who helped us win our class in the Bermuda Race in 1990, was a seasoned navigator, a veteran of seven iterations of that ocean race, and also of other contests and adventures along both the Eastern Seaboard, and the coasts of Japan, where he was a war correspondent during the days of the Vietnam conflict. He taught many of us less seasoned sailors the arts of celestial navigation, from the calibration of a sextant to the establishment of a fix. But Sid had not crossed the Atlantic and would have come gladly with us were not for his busy schedule working for Dow Jones. During the summer of 1991, he set some time aside to come and sail the Mediterranean on *Pirate*.

In Portugal we had a change of watch: Simon Wynn, our Atlantic navigator, went home, and Sid arrived in Lisbon, where he joined us, and we travelled south to Vilamoura. He came with starry Hollywood expectations: he had visions of a dapper Cary Grant in the Riviera cruising on calm blue waters with gentle breezes wafting the yacht along. On *Pirate* it wasn't quite that way. He recorded this in the log:

> *The weather is considerably different...virtually no clouds or rain, at least not in midsummer. Instead of air masses and fronts, as we know the weather to be at home [New York], there are large imbalances in air pressure caused by differences in temperatures over the African deserts and the European continent. These lead to strong flows of air with no apparent reason. That of course means wind...we constantly experienced sudden strong blasts of wind out of absolutely clear skies. And these frequently continued for days before petering out...completely.*

I wished to take *Pirate* from Portugal to Greece, where she would spend the winter under the protection of friends and partners in Athens. This meant a delivery trip on a tight schedule, rather than a cruise. The voyage, comprising almost the entire length of the Mediterranean, did not include many of the glamorous ports, nor time for sightseeing.

Like many places that are widely known, the Mediterranean is beset by misconceptions. For offshore sailors, this inner sea lacks the prestige of larger oceans. Its waters and shores evoke many pleasures, but not challenging passages. And yet they are wrong. It is a beautiful *and* difficult sea.

There are two gates to the Mediterranean, the Pillars of Hercules in the West, and the Hellespont in the East. At each of them, Europe asserts itself and completes itself. As Marguerite Yourcenar wrote "East and West have, for twenty centuries, oscillated like the two ends of a seesaw, whose fulcrum is Rome. As in the Greek archipelago, empires are won or lost here as the result of sudden squalls and the risk of combat at close quarters: Spain has Trafalgar, in the way the Levant has Actium or Lepanto."[4] Back and forth, on *Pirate* we rode the seasaw three times, and sailed above the wreckage of warships in Lepanto (today Naphpaktos—Ναύπακτος) and Trafalgar—the latter with Bonaparte on board, our English Springer Spaniel.

Sailing in the Med consists of motoring between gales. Each area has its own peculiar winds. These local blows are so distinct, each has its own name: *levanter, sci-rocco, meltemi, gregale, libeccio, tramontana, vendavales*, and so on.

On *Pirate* we became familiar with the *levanter* early on. It is an easterly wind that howls through the Strait of Gibraltar separating Spain from Morocco. As we approached the strait we found the waters at the Gulf of Cadiz increasingly turbulent. By the time we got near Trafalgar we shortened sail but took a terrible beating. The *levanter* was blowing Force 9: a strong gale with 45-knot winds, high waves, rolling seas, dense streaks of foam, and a spray that reduced visibility. We ran for safety to the port of Cadiz where we were holed up for three days until the winds subsided. Tied up alongside us at the Royal Yacht Club in Cadiz was a 28-foot sloop sailed by a Swedish couple. They were so discouraged that they sold their boat in Spain and returned home by train. For them, as for the ancients, Cadiz was Ultima Gades, the gateway to the Atlantic, and the end of their adventures.

Because the Mediterranean, unlike the Atlantic, is an endless shore rather than an endless sea, and because long periods of calm alternate with furious gales, the vessels that navigated its waters since time immemorial were never fully sailing vessels. Boats need other means of propulsion: today a motor—in ancient times, the oars. Phoenicians, Persians, Greeks, Romans, Arabs, Genoese, Venetians, Ottoman Turks, and Maltese propelled their vessels with blades, often manned by slaves, with sails used only as auxiliary power.

The civilizations of the Mediterranean were all coastal civilizations. They extended only a few hundred miles inland. The sea was a constant presence. The mountains looked on the cities, and the cities looked on the sea. Meat and milk come from the slopes, while olives, grapes, wheat, and vegetables come from the plains and terraces.

[4] Marguerite Yourcenar, *That Mighty Sculptor, Time*; The Noonday Press, New York: 1992; p.159, translated by Walter Kaiser.

From one end of the Med to the other, there are many local disturbances that make sailing a puzzle, and weather forecasts a guess. The most adverse feature is the summer draught, ruled by the Sahara, and made worse every year by climate change. During the long and hot summer months, the basin is cut off from the north and the west. In the winter, which is always milder than on the continent, cyclones break through from the Atlantic and there is rain, cloudy weather, and some formidable storms. But during the summer, when most people sail for pleasure, sunny days do not mean the absence of bad weather. Nothing is more disconcerting than Force 9 winds from cloudless skies.

As for the water, the Mediterranean has unique characteristics of evaporation and salinity. The Med may be described as a deep oval pan, 2,300 miles long and 500 miles at its widest point. Geological upheavals produced thousands of islands and peninsulas, and the erosion of the shores turned the coastline into a ragged edge. Place the pan under a broiler called the sun, and you get a lot of surface evaporation. Although the Med is connected to the Atlantic by a narrow strait, the colder ocean does not mitigate the high temperature. The Med retains an average temperature 18 degrees higher than the Atlantic, and is the hottest of all seas in the temperate zones.

When the *levanter* abated, *Pirate* aimed her bow towards Gibraltar. Across the strait, only 13 miles away, we could see the Rock's twin pillar, Mount Hacko on the North African coast. Many centuries ago, the pillars marked the gate that separated the known world from the unknown. Today Gibraltar is an odd mixture of human and baboon, of Spaniard and Briton, of military and civilian, of patrol boats and drug smugglers, of the pretentious and the honky-tonk. Sailors still favor "the Gib" because of its good chandleries, fine mechanics, reasonable prices, and the English language. We spent a couple of days there, getting supplies and minor repairs.

From Gibraltar to the Balearic Islands our cruise was warm and windless. We motored along the barren coast of Spain, formerly a desert, now beset by modern tourist developments. In Spain and Portugal these developments were made possible by funds from the European Community. Easy money and greed led to over-building, and the result was a series of Potemkin villages waiting for tourists that failed to come. Where such developments succeeded, the result was no less sad: polluted waters, beaches full of trash, and endless stands of junk food. At the other end of the Mediterranean, in Greece the same EU funds were not applied or "disappeared," and as a result, many of the beautiful islands were left unspoiled. Ironically, thwarted development had kept Greece authentic, and its little ports quite quaint.

From Torrevieja we sailed towards Ibiza and Formentera, where we did not stay long, since we had a scheduled rendezvous in Sardinia with friends from New York. Headwinds forced us to sail southward to within 90 miles of the Algerian coast. At that distance we were struck by a *sirocco* that covered the sails with red sand from the desert. The *sirocco* is a sickening wind. It originates as a warm dry wind but picks up moisture over the sea. It mixes vapor with the sand. Then it makes white sails bleed. The pilot book for the area read, "It is said that if the *sirocco* blows for more than ten days all crimes of passion and violence are ascribed to the weather and their perpetrators excused." It was an apt introduction to the wilder side of Sardinia and Sicily.

The leg from Ibiza to Cagliari was a straight shot of 360 hard miles. There was nothing there in the Sardo-Balearic Abbyssal Plain—no traffic, no human or marine life. Near the shores of Sardinia land breezes brought a scent of pine, and life seemed sweeter. Cagliari, the capital, is a busy commercial port, and a city of honest charm. Once in port we met our anxious New York friends, less patient on land with their urban schedules than we were at sea with finicky winds. The entry formalities were perfunctory, and my Italian made them faster, I think. I even became a member of the Lega Navale Italiana, Sezione Cagliari.

At the end of July, *Pirate* left Sardinia and crossed the Sicilian channel towards Malta. Despite the terrible reputation of those waters in a gale, our passage was smooth, driven by a gentle northwest breeze. The night watch was intoxicating; the moon was full and the skies clear. I hoisted the light drifter and listened to Luciano Pavarotti singing arias while the ship hissed along the waves. We left the Egadi Islands to port on the night of July 28. The next day we sailed closer to the shore, hoping to catch a glimpse of Agrigentum, the great archaeological park of Magna Grecia. It was hidden by the haze, so imagined but not seen. The morning of July 30 we sighted Gozo, the northernmost island of the Maltese group.

We were intercepted by an armed patrol boat, which seemed reluctantly satisfied with our declared intention to make port in Marsamxett. We almost ran aground in the shallow bay of Sliema, thinking it was our harbor. We corrected the lapse and changed course just in time. The episode taught me how tensions among the crew, distraction, fatigue, and an unknown shore can put a boat on the rocks, on a clear day, under ideal sailing conditions, and after 4,000 miles of uneventful crossings. But the gods were kind and we arrived safely in what the Phoenicians called Malet—the Safe Haven, the Hiding Place.

The island of Malta is situated at the very center of the Mediterranean, and has arguably the best harbor in that sea. Because of that, Malta was destined to be the site of terrible battles, sieges, clashes of cultures and of faiths. Few places on earth have witnessed human carnage with such regularity. During World War II, it was incessantly bombed. For resisting the air and sea raids by the Axis powers, King George VI bestowed the George Cross to the islanders, and Franklin Roosevelt issued a presidential citation for bravery. Royal Navy Captain Ernle Bradford in *Malta Invicta,* tells the story on the pages of *National Geographic*, March 1943.

In 1565, Malta withstood a terrible siege by the Ottoman Turks. Suleiman the Magnificent, Sultan of the Ottoman Empire, had driven the Knights of St. John out of the island of Rhodes, where they had settled after being forced to leave Palestine. Now he wanted them out of the Mediterranean completely. The fighting in Malta raged for four months. Some 30,000 Turks were killed, while of the 9,000 defenders, only 600 were left. The Turkish troops were under the command of a famous corsair named Dragut. The Knights were led by Grand Master Jean Parissot de la Valette. Both commanders were septuagenarians and both had toiled as galley slaves to one another. At one point, Dragut had all captured knights and the bodies of those already fallen decapitated. Then he floated the headless bodies on wooden crosses to the defenders across a channel. The Grand Master responded in kind by ordering all Turkish prisoners beheaded, and had their heads volleyed back across the water from his cannons. In the end the Knights prevailed, and thus stopped the westward advance of the Ottomans. In recognition of this feat, Emperor Charles V gave the islands to the knights. In return, the knights had to pay the emperor an annual fee of one falcon, since falconry was their favorite sport. The legend of the Maltese Falcon was born.

Today Malta is perhaps a kinder place, although the local Museum of Fine Arts displays a large collection of violent martyrdom. Piracy and mischief are dormant but not dead. From the moment of our arrival, we felt thwarted and observed. Both government and civil society seemed to be about watching and controlling. Several intermediaries brokered every service and transaction, and we felt surrounded by spies.

Most of *Pirate*'s crew had to get back home. They left Sid and me, navigator and skipper, alone in Malta to complete the boat's voyage to Greece. It seemed prudent to search for crew. Through one of the many broker services in port, I found a willing young man, with proper references, ready to sail with us. From then on it would be just three men on the boat, across the Ionian Sea.

The wind—a seasonal but unusually strong *maestrale*—made us fly on a broad reach. In just three days we reached the island of Kythira, stunning in its silent dignity, where legend has it that Aphrodite was born. When Paris absconded with Helen in Sparta, the lovers stopped in Kythira on their way to Troy. Kythira was a colony of Minoan Crete, then a pirate stronghold in the Middle Ages, and was taken by the Venetians in 1717. Its subsequent history followed that of the Ionian Islands, including the British protectorate, and union with Greece in 1864. In our own times, a large portion of the population migrated to Australia, to which the locals refer as "big Kythira."

Our hired sailor did not know all this. He was surly, moody, and ill behaved. I asked myself whether I had put a murderous psychopath on board. So I made it plain to him that he had to obey, that only I knew the way, that my connections in Greece were powerful, that they knew our schedule and course, and that his very fate depended on my good will. I had never acted as a capo mafioso before, but this time I made the young man an offer he could not refuse. It worked. Henceforth, he was resentful but meek. Henceforth too, I treated him generously, as Machiavelli recommends: add rewards, not insult, to injury. Besides, his brawn if not his brain was useful to me. Ten days later, after I had sent him back to Malta with a plane ticket, and I rested in beautiful Santorini, a Greek professional captain told me, as if it were a fact of nature, "nobody hires crew in Malta!"

From Kythira, it was a straight shot to Hydra, past ominous Cape Malea (the

Cape Horn of the Med) to port and through the shipping lanes. We left in the afternoon and spent a sleepless night on watch as tanker after tanker, container ship after ship passed us in both directions. We arrived in Hydra early the following afternoon. As in Kythira, we were "tolerated" for an overnight stay, but still had not officially entered Greece. We ate lobster and visited the elegant town, pleasant without cars; only donkeys and mules were allowed.

We had one more day of sailing before reaching our destination: a berth in Zea Marina, in Piraeus. As we approached Athens, I pointed to the right of our bow with an operatic gesture; there in the hazy distance, was the Acropolis, and in front, the Parthenon. *"Greece! The scent and the taste, the Honey of metamorphoses, all Greece; serpent and dove, rude and gentle, secluded and open, all at once."* —From Leo Bronstein, *Romantic Homage to Greece and Spain*; New Brunswick and London: Transaction Publishers. 1993; p. 20.

Pirate and I were in Greece at last—in many ways a second home.

The last hurdle was the authorities. It was Friday, late in the afternoon, and whoever was left on duty was unwilling and surly. But *Pirate*'s guardian angels soon appeared, and we were allowed to dock, get water, and use a telephone. The computer on board had counted all the sea miles since we left Jamestown in Rhode Island: 4,992 miles. I did not wait until a round 5,000 to get very drunk that night.

Summer passed and winter came—in Greece there are only two seasons! *Pirate* stayed moored at Microlimano, a small yacht port in Piraeus, and I flew back to New York. I had to work, and teach, and prepare the next adventure.

Back in Athens, *Pirate* had entered an ancient world. There the present blends with history, and history with myth. Behold the Aegean, and as D.H. Lawrence said:

> *They are not dead, they are not dead!*
> *[...] The dawn is not off the sea, and Odysseus' ships*
> *have not yet passed the islands. I must watch them still.*
> —D.H. Lawrence, "The Argonauts," *Last Poems* (1933).

Was the *Odyssey* the account of a real voyage or a magnificent fairy tale? What about Odysseus' voyage, the wind, the vessel, and the sea? Only sailors in small boats can seek to answer questions about the likelihood of the story. The British naval officer,

Ernle Bradford, sought to reconstruct the legendary voyage in his book *Ulysses Found,* and found it perfectly credible. The winds, the shores, the rhythms of the sea are all still there. But the most amazing thing is that the character of the story is still with us: Western man as sailorman—crafty, adaptable, inventive, bent on profit, a taker of risks, dominant and strong, and winner in the end. The Greeks call him *polimichanos* (πολυμήχανος), the all-resourceful.

Pirate found an all-resourceful sailor to protect her in the same small harbor where the black ships of Odysseus once beached. Manolis was his name. He remembered sailing his own 12-foot dinghy when he was six years old, against his father's wishes. Ever since then he sailed boats, made sails, fitted out yachts, raced, made it to the Olympics, taught, fished, and passed all this knowledge to his son, to local seamen, and to sailors from distant lands, like me, and many other friends. His home was near Piraeus, in a small port bordered by a string of taverns. It has an oval shape and many names: *Microlimano,* Fanari, Tourkolimano, or Koumoundourou port. It was called Koumoundourou because of the namesake mansion at its south end, where the Nautical Club of *Greece* stands today.

Boats lay in and out of the water, in all seasons, and in all states of care or disrepair. The buildings that surrounded that quiet fleet were the sheds of two sailing clubs, a parking lot, the workshops of a carpenter and a welder, and at the end a tavern called *The Black Goat* (Μαύρη Γίδα). The sailors that hung out there had accumulated as many years of sailing as Greece was old. When they finished work on a boat, and they liked the result, they grilled sardines and drank wine in the shadow of her hull. Manolis stood out among the sailors of that group for the same reasons that put Odysseus in command of the ancient ships: the knowledge, the seamanship, the ruses and the tricks, the daring solution to a stubborn problem that in the end, unbelievably, worked. His grandfather was in the Greek navy, and his father built and raced his own yacht (the family boats were called *Dream,* "Ονειροι" *I* and *II*). Manolis grew up in that small harbor where everybody sailed, dogs included. Manolis' dog was called αναρχία (*Anarchy*). For those two, the only authority was the mighty sea.

When summer came in May, Manolis trained part of *Pirate*'s crew in the arts of hoisting, dousing, and messing up spinnakers, even broaching, until all of us lost our fear of those sails. In June, *Pirate* was fit to roam the world. Christina arrived in Athens, and so did sailing friends from as far as San Diego, New York, and Caracas. Staggered in nice bunches, they crewed on our boat in a happy two-month tour of the Aegean. The high points were the islands of Skiros, Chios, Samos, Patmos, and the very special Santorini. Many were the magic moments, like the evening in which we anchored under the temple of Poseidon in Cape Sounion, next to the J-Class, *Endeavour.*

The visit to Chios was significant because it is the island where Columbus, then a young seaman on Genoese merchant ships, learned to sail. With this stop-over, *Pirate* became the only boat in the 1992 America 500 fleet to have reached the very source of the Columbian saga, where a young man from Genoa would fulfill Seneca's prophetic lines:

> *There will come in the late years of the world*
> *certain times in which the Ocean will wash over*
> *the land and a great land will be opened and a new*
> *mariner resembling Jason, named Typhis, will*
> *discover a new world, and the island Thule*
> *will no longer be the farthest point on earth.*[5]

In Patmos, we visited the Monastery of the Apocalypse. A small cave there gave shelter to St. John the Evangelist, exiled in 95 A.D. by the Roman Emperor Domitian. Here John had a vision of "the things which are, and the things which shall be hereafter." (*Revelation*, Chapter 1, verses 12-16.)

Santorini was a marvelous surprise for the crew, and a special homecoming for me, who had been there several times before. In Serifos we were trapped by a gale—the *meltemi* winds had arrived. It was a hard sail back to Athens.

Pirate wintered in Microlimano, the little yacht port in Piraeus. I had to take a long flight from New York every time I wished to putter below decks. The only mishap was in March, when *Pirate* was cast adrift from her mooring by two youngsters; they broke in one night looking for drugs, but finding none, stole the flares and some

[5] Seneca, *Medea* p.375-79.

The Skipper in Santorini

Patagonia fleeces instead. They neglected to properly secure their boarding dinghy, lost it, cut the mooring line in a panic, drifted to another boat, and from there ran ashore. *Pirate* was rescued by a fisherman, and so came out unscathed. In June 1992, she was ready for sea again, all the way back to Gibraltar.

That summer, with a different set of friends, we left Greece through the Corinth Canal. In the Gulf of Corinth we made three visits. First came the city itself, modern and nondescript. We then visited Galaxidia, a beautiful 19th century town. It became the stepping-stone of our pilgrimage to the sacred oracle of Delphi. Finally we visited Naphpaktos, the site of the decisive battle of Lepanto, where a soldier of fortune named Miguel de Cervantes y Saavedra lost one hand by the shot of an harquebus. Thereafter he used his other hand to write *Don Quixote de la Mancha*.

Juan and Christina

History and myth came alive again. In Delphi, we remembered that once the oracle saved Greece, and it had to do with ships. There was a time when the Persian conquest of the Greeks was almost assured. The Athenians however, decided to resist. They sent envoys to Delphi, where the priestess uttered some terrifying words, full of bad omens. Undeterred, the Athenians entered the temple a second time, bearing gifts, and asked for a new prophecy. The prophetess, who did not shy from bribes by the determined, then uttered a revised version, which said:

> *Yet Zeus the all-seeing grants Athena's prayer*
> *that the wooden wall only shall not fall, but help*
> *you and your children.*

The Athenians took the wooden wall to mean ships, and put all their efforts into the preparation of their fleet. They met the invaders by sea, beat them in the battle of Salamis, and saved Greece. The battle could have turned otherwise, in which case, if we are to believe the great German sociologist, Max Weber, the very fate of the West would have been neither free nor democratic, but despotic and theocratic.

After the Gulf of Corinth, we visited the Homeric islands of the Ionian Sea. Our last port of call was Levkas, which some believe was the original Ithaca of Homeric fame. Ithaca was the home of Odysseus, whose delayed return to the island is the plot of the classical Greek tale the *Odyssey.* My own Ithaca—the site of a forever postponed homecoming—was thousands of miles away, in Buenos Aires, on the muddy shores of the River Plate. With the poet Konstantin Cavafy, I believe each person has their own Ithaca to accomplish:

Always keep Ithaca fixed in your mind.
To arrive there is your ultimate goal.
But do not hurry the voyage at all.
It is better to let it last for long years;
And even to anchor at the isle when you are old,
Rich with all that you have gained on the way,
Not expecting that Ithaca will offer you riches.

Ithaca has given you the beautiful voyage.
Without her you would never have taken the road.
But she has nothing more to give you.

And if you find her poor, Ithaca has not defrauded you.
With the great wisdom you have gained, with so much experience,
You must surely have understood by then what these Ithacas mean.[6]

[6] Source: C.P. *Cavafy: Collected Poems*; Princeton University Press, NJ: 1975.

We crossed over to Italy, passing between the rock of Scylla and the whirlpool of Charybdis (three times in my life I have crossed these treacherous straits on small boats), anchoring under the volcano of Stromboli, which saluted us three times with fireworks. The volcano honored its ancient fame as the brightest lighthouse of the Med. We touched Porto Cervo in Sardinia, before crossing over to Corsica, to anchor in Porto Vecchio, Bonifacio, and Propriano. From Corsica we sailed to the Balearic Islands of Spain. We loved Mahon in Minorca, and also Palma in Mallorca, where we arrived in time to watch the King's Cup. We then crossed to the coast of mainland Spain, avoided the Olympics in Barcelona, and hopped from port to port until we saw the Rock of Gibraltar. We did not stop until we reached the Atlantic again.

It was quite a glorious summer, but we left the Mediterranean with a sense of relief, for it is—as Bernard Moitessier said in *Cap Horn à la voile*—a most fatiguing sea. Past Trafalgar, we breathed deeper. In musical terms, I like to think of the Mediterranean as Vivaldi: nice but choppy—and of the Atlantic as Beethoven: majestic and sublime.

Nineteen people came on board as crew in our Mediterranean crossing, meeting *Pirate* in some pre-determined port of call, and leaving in another. To schedule them appropriately required considerable coordination, but it went without a hitch. During the last 700 miles, *Pirate* had only Christina, Bonaparte, and me as the crew. All of us—ship and trio—enjoyed it immensely, even counting the gales, the rocks, and Napoleonic wrecks off Cape Trafalgar. We were back on the ocean, and its promise of a different sort of navigation, with an ever-receding horizon and long daily runs. We finally rested in a slip at Puerto Sherry, and awaited the arrival of the America 500 fleet, which we were ready to join.

6

Voyages of Discovery

It is easy to discover
what another has discovered before.

—Christopher Columbus

America 500 was a special transatlantic event, both a rally and a race, which commemorated the 500th anniversary of Christopher Columbus' voyage to the New World in 1492. It was the second of three quincentennial sailing events across the Atlantic. The first was the Great Columbus Regatta in June 1992, in which most of the tall ships of the world participated, as well as modern ocean racers.

The second was the Discovery Route, with many state-of-the-art maxis and Whitbread boats, which started in Puerto Sherry (Bay of Cadiz) on November 28, and finished in Miami in mid-December. The third one was the America 500, in which *Pirate* participated. It started in Palos, Andalusia, and ended in San Salvador, in the Bahamas. Of these three races, the America 500 followed most closely the route taken by the three caravels, the *Niña*, the *Pinta*, and the *Santa Maria*. It was the event most laden with official ceremony, symbolic stopovers, and controversy regarding racing rules. It involved 147 sailing yachts from 22 countries.

From ancient times, the Greeks had vaguely situated the Garden of Hesperides somewhere in the south of Spain, and beyond the coast of Spain, their Island of Heroes. They were mythical places, but they would soon become geographical. It was only after Columbus, at the very end of the fifteenth century, and later, during the reign of Charles V, that the Atlantic became the Ocean Sea, its islands became better known, and a new continent was given a name.

In the days prior to the start, the sailors visited many places associated with Columbus. The skippers of the modern yachts were briefed on August 2 in the Monastery of La Rábida in the same room where Columbus briefed his captains. All sailors signed a commemorative book at the Columbus monument, at the junction of the Rivers Tinto and Odiel. A mass and a blessing of the fleet were held at dawn on August 3 in the Church of Saint George, just as they were held for the Genovese admiral half a millennium before, and for his jealous Spanish captains with their motley crews. (I will not dwell on the ethnic cleansing of Moors and Jews that took place at the same time and from the same spot, who were forcefully sent away on other ships, a fact that delayed Columbus planned departure from Palos.)

After review by the King and Queen of Spain, the modern sailors went down in procession to the spot where the caravels had been moored in 1492. On August 3, 1992, a first fleet of 50 yachts set sail from Palos de la Frontera.

The first fleet of yachts raced from Palos to Porto Santo, a small volcanic island in the Madeira archipelago where Columbus had lived for several years with his first wife, and where he first drew up the plans for his expedition. There Columbus met a moribund Portuguese pilot, who had been shipwrecked in the Antilles and somehow made it back to Madeira, to whisper the news of land across the ocean in Columbus' ears, before dying in his arms. In Porto Santo a monument was unveiled to commemorate the America 500 fleet. The monument is made of concrete and steel in the shape of a sail. From Porto Santo the fleet sailed to Funchal, the capital of Madeira, and from Madeira the fleet raced to the Canary Islands, where a program of events had been organized, sponsored by the local government. It included a rally around the seven Canary Islands.

A second, more numerous fleet of 75 yachts left Palos on October 12 and followed an identical program. *Pirate* was in this second fleet. This time the weather turned nasty, and boats had to brave strong head winds and breaking seas. Those of us who belonged to the second fleet had to lick our wounds (some sails were torn, and other gear went bust in a gale) in the relative calm of the Canaries. The two fleets came together in Las Palmas de Gran Canaria to prepare for the mass start of the transatlantic leg on November 15, 1992.

My own preparations for America 500 started in 1989, when I acquired *Pirate*. I was determined to take her across the Atlantic, so that I could sail her back to America in 1992—even if my blue water experience was limited—even if such a voyage was not "politically correct." Why? Maybe because I was born on October 12, maybe because as a child I was enthralled by Columbus' story, maybe because my ancestors had sailed from Genoa to Buenos Aires in the 19th century. When the first Corradis arrived in Argentina in the 1850s, the harbor of Buenos Aires was not suitable for ocean-going ships. The water was so shallow that ships had to anchor several miles out, and they were loaded and unloaded by means of flat-bottom lighters. Passengers were transferred from the ship to a lighter, then to a mule-driven cart, and sometimes they were carried ashore on the back of a rugged man. That was one of a Corradi's first job in Argentina. I can picture him: a latter-day Christopher, a stormy Genoese, swearing that the man on his back was the heaviest he had ever carried, demanding an exorbitant fee. I would do the crossing, in short, because I had it in my blood.

With this idea in mind, I had prepared *Pirate* from the start for long ocean passages. I entered *Pirate* in the 1990 Bermuda Race, as described before, as a serious test of the boat's and the crew's abilities. A seasoned Australian sailor and friend, Simon Wynn, helped in organizing the crew. Our victory in Bermuda boosted morale and gave new impetus to the transatlantic project. I decided to sail from Rhode Island to Portugal and Spain. Since my Greek friends, Annika and Manos were so busy that they seldom came for a sail on *Pirate*, I decided to sail across the Mediterranean, and to moor the boat at their doorstep in Athens. This was accomplished in the summer of 1991. It was truly grand to cruise on such a vast scale: 5,000 nautical miles, six countries, six languages, 13 seaports, 63 days, in all kinds of seas, as described in detail in previous chapters. Yet the adventures of 1990 and 1991 were a prologue to the

Columbian homecoming of 1992.

In Spain, *Pirate* was hauled out and pampered with a new coat of bottom paint, a thorough cleaning of her topsides, an engine tune-up, a check of the rig, the installation of a watermaker, and a new boom vang, while Christina and I took care of other business in Paris and New York. A month later we returned to southern Spain, where we were joined by Bill and Helen De Neergaard, Corinthians from New York, and Yoli Magee from Athens, for the first two legs of the America 500 rally.

The port of San Lucar de Barrameda, from which the first caravels and later the galleons steered their course westward; the monastery of La R*á*bida, where Columbus and his captains received their charges to sail the Ocean Sea; the archives of Seville, where everything that happended afterwards in the Americas was recorded—all of these places I had visited in my readings as a child: with Walter Scott and Emilio Salgari, Jack London and Mark Twain, and a 20-volume encyclopedia titled *El tesoro de la juventud*. I had traveled far and wide: I had the greatest adventures without leaving a big armchair in my parents' *jardin d'hiver*. These became real in 1992, as real as the vessel that I was steering westward, and as real as the waves of the Ocean Sea which I was about to brave.

Our fleet left Puerto Sherry on October 9, 1992, in a fun race to the Andalusian port of Huelva. In Huelva we anchored 12 miles up the Odiel River. In 1492 Columbus had anchored nearby, in the Tinto River, which has silted up since then, and is now inaccessible because of a low bridge. The tides, the current, and the wind work at cross-purposes, and they wreck havoc with anchors and chains.

When we finally departed in the afternoon of October 12 with all ships fully dressed and moving solemnly on parade past Columbus' monument, it was also my 49th birthday—my only birthday marked with a salvo of cannon fire. It seemed to me an auspicious and fiery celebration of middle age. In 1492, Columbus wrote in his log: "We set sail on this day, from the bar of Saltes. A strong sea wind bore us sixty miles to the south, which is fifteen leagues; then southwest and south by west, which was the course for the Canary Islands…"

Our first leg of the America 500, the stretch between Huelva and Porto Santo in Madeira, was roughly equivalent to the distance between Newport and Bermuda—and the passage was equally boisterous. The skies were gray; the winds were light and variable at first, but two days into the passage, the glass dropped and the breeze freshened. *Pirate* found herself facing stiff winds from the westerly quarter. On October 15, we entered a tropical depression. We had a rough ride, with 30 knots of wind on the nose, stiff waves, line squalls, thunder, lightning, and heavy rain. These ghoulish forces were followed by periods of calm, but with ugly lingering seas—what the French call *la mer morte.* Then came more squalls, and so on until we crossed the finish line in the small hours of October 18, tired, penalized for passing one of the (dark) buoys on the wrong side, and with an MOB episode to cap it all.

The man went overboard when we were dousing the mainsail, when one of the crew released his harness, lost his step, and went into the sea. Luckily, the recovery procedure took only five minutes. So we had the good fortune to arrive in one piece. Not the Nautor mast, which managed to shake loose the neoprene wedges that held it in place where it goes through the deck. A wobbly mast can be scary, but is a nuisance common to most classic Swans, and it can easily be set right with a lot of winching and some ingenuity: better done in port than at sea. There we had a crowd of knowledgeable sailors, all willing to help.

As always, it was not the wind that proved troublesome, but the seas that punished hulls, rigs, and sailors. Other boats in the fleet did not fare as well. There were several dismastings. A Tayana 37 was dismasted after broaching under spinnaker and her skipper motored to port. A Nonsuch catboat from Louisiana also lost its—unsupported—mast. The crew motored all the way to Las Palmas where they found an ingenious replacement: a wooden mast from an impounded boat that the Spanish Red Cross had been using as a flagpole! In the entire rally from Huelva to the Bahamas, five boats lost their masts, and there were scores of torn sails. There was one abandoned ship: the Argentinian 42' sloop *Mano Brava,* with a broken rudder and a serious leak. The crew abandoned the vessel and was picked up by another yacht, but *Mano Brava* survived and was salvaged later, and towed to Funchal, the capital of Madeira. Line honors in the Palos to Porto Santo leg went to a Finnish maxi designed by German Frers. On corrected time, the winner was a much smaller Finnish yacht, a Comfortina 38 built in Sweden.

We found the small island of Porto Santo simple, barren, yet full of charm; in Columbus' days, it was covered with pines. The governor of the island and the mayor of the port town received the skippers with honors. They signed our log books in the council chamber, an old building fronting the main square, which also housed a small whitewashed church dating from before Columbus' era. There was a reception at a house where Columbus is thought to have lived for a while, featuring Madeira wine and sweet cake. That house is now a museum celebrating Columbus "as a young family man," and featuring the usual paraphernalia of ship models, charts, quadrants and astrolabes.

The sail from Porto Santo to Funchal in the main island of Madeira was pleasant, and the reception lovely. We appreciated the spirit of Finn sailors aboard *Sea Face* and *Funstar*. They were serious racers as well as compassionate good men. We did not mind the crowded dirty harbor. The place exuded Portuguese sweet charm. Inside, the island impresses the visitor with its luxuriant vegetation and the intense cultivation of its terraces. Banana plantations, vineyards, vegetable gardens, flower markets, spectacular views from mountain tops, cliffs over the ocean, and high cascades make Madeira a unique wonderland with a life of its own, far beyond the functions of tourism and retirement.

At an outdoor reception for the fleet, a downpour dispersed the crowd. Christina and I found refuge under an improvised tent where we met the commander of the port. We spent most of the night with him, enjoying *fados* sung by the commander and his friends in a downtown club, and at his house. As mentioned before, *fados* are haunting and melancholy songs about life at sea and long-lost love, made famous by performers such as Dulce Pontes, Ondeia Musica, Canção do Mar, Amalia Rodgrigues, Barco Negro. That evening alone made our ocean passage worthwhile.

After a long session of *fados* and drinks, we still found energy to start the race to the Canaries the next day. It was a wallop and a gallop. We left in the evening with winds of 20 knots on the beam. *Pirate* flew past boat after boat into a raucous night. Morning caught us sailing on a broad reach, over-canvassed, at a steady clip of eight knots, with 20-foot following seas. The wind gusted to Force 8. White crests cascaded down the wave faces. With 40 knots from astern, working headsail and a reef in the main, we had a few bad gybes but managed to avoid any breaks. It was Atlantic sailing at its best on a sturdy Swan: hard, fast, wet, and exhilarating. It was also dangerous because the following seas were destructive, and the crew quite tired and not a little alarmed. In the end, the waves managed to overtake the syphon in the exhaust and swamped the engine.

After crossing the finish line long before anyone else in the class, I realized that it would be hard to come into the port of Arrecife in a gale without power. To play it safe, I radioed Puerto Calero, in the isle of Lanzarote, some 10 miles to the south, where nice people in the marina agreed to give us a tow. Unfortunately they did it at high speed. We avoided a crash but still scratched the topsides on the dock. Nevertheless we managed to save the flooded engine after draining and washing it with fresh water and diesel.

So far, the America 500 had been rough: in each leg, a gale. Boats and crews needed some tender love and care. With other boats we lingered in a great marina, and visited the uncanny sights of the volcanic island of Lanzarote. Within the fleet, a small fleet of Swans, 65, 46, and 38s, cruised the south of Lanzarote and the north of Fuerteventura, and thence we sailed to Tenerife. We had a lot of fun at anchor and visited other boats. One sunny morning, off the island of Lobos, the largest of the Swans, the 65' *Show Me*, hosted the crews from the other boats for a hearty brunch, followed by a "beautiful legs" contest: all the men aboard had to show their legs, and the women formed the jury of the hairy and muscular exhibition.

Tenerife is a large, majestic island. El Teide, one of the tallest active volcanoes on earth, crowns it. We docked at the port of Radazul, a few miles south of the busy port of Santa Cruz. Finally, on American Election Day, we sailed to our gathering port of Las Palmas de Gran Canaria. I bid farewell to *Pirate*'s crew up to that point, and to Christina, who had other business to attend. The days that followed were busy with repairs and provisions. The list was endless but made easier with a number of sailors I befriended: a taxi driver, an electrician, and a welder. One of them, a Frenchman from Brittany, allowed me to use his sail loft to manufacture a spinnaker net. Brookes & Gatehouse sent their top instrument man from London to inspect the electronics, and to repair or replace them at little cost.

Meanwhile the new crew arrived from different latitudes: Argentina, Greece, and the US. They were in great spirits, and eager to race across the Atlantic. The four friends had left jobs and families behind and they brought, besides the intangible wish to win, concrete things with them: a new mainsail cut in Hong Kong, boat gear, personal kits, and some provisions as well. My cousin Alejandro Maloberti from Buenos Aires, Manolis Pantelis from Athens, Bro Uttal and Simon Wynn from America. Most of them had sailed on *Pirate* before. We formed a middle-aged, international, and polyglot bunch: skipper, navigator, tactician, cook, and trimmer. English was our *lingua franca* on board, peppered with occasional dialogues in Spanish, and frequent blasphemies in Greek.

In an ocean rally that spans several months and thousands of sea miles in several legs, it is unrealistic to expect the same crew to stay for the duration. The ocean race becomes a long theater play that only the director knows from beginning to end, while actors come and go with every act. Only boat and skipper are bonded *sine die*. And yet through it all a community spirit prevailed. We made mistakes but corrected them, and learned from them. The equipment performed well. Mishaps occurred: we blew two spinnakers which we repaired underway, lost a halyard and made Manolis climb the mast to retrieve it in the middle of the passage, and we broke a spinnaker pole against the shrouds—luckily we carried two poles. Communications worked well, and the engine did not fail to charge the batteries. *Pirate* was heavy and stressed, but kept giving us miles at good speed. Through the high seas operator, the SSB radio brought on board the sound of the familiar voices of wives, parents, and even travel agents from places as far away as France, the American west coast, New York, and Buenos Aires. In each long leg of the rally, the radio net was run daily and positions were reported to Rally Control. The net gave the participants a sense of camaraderie, which was real, and a sense of safety, which can be misleading, especially if it relaxes proper vigilance and seamanship. A few emergencies were reported through the net and help was delivered.

While we were crossing the Atlantic, we learned that a sailor from Rhode Island whom I had met in Jamestown, Mike Plant, was lost at sea on his way to the start of the Vendée Globe Challenge in Les Sables d'Olonne, France. On November 22, his boat *Coyote* was found capsized some 500 miles north of the Azores with a partially inflated life raft still lashed to the pulpit. Another racer, Nigel Burgess, was also lost, probably while trying to board the life raft from his flooding vessel, and the boom struck him. Unlike Plant's, his body was found a few days later. One's last day at sea may be a short day, in which a series of banal accidents cascades into swift doom. Mishaps and errors at sea always come in chains. In my log I wrote: "Better to pass boldly into that other world in the full glory of some passion than fade and wither dismally with age." Burgess and Plant are in the company of Slocum and Tabarly, and so many other sailing comrades who died doing what they loved.

On board *Pirate,* we had trivial problems, some of them hilarious. Sailing before the wind under various spinnakers, day and night, and often surfing on big waves, actually reversed the self-bailing system of the cockpit. Instead of draining water, the scuppers brought it in. We were riding a bidet on the high seas!

We chose a system of staggered watches: two men on deck at all times, alternating between driving and trimming every one and a half hours, with a fresh replacement thereafter. The system allowed everyone to stand watch for three hours, to share a watch with everyone else, and to get enough rest in between. It also allowed for continuity between watches. The skipper and the tactician however, were on call at all times. When a sail change was required, or something urgent needed attention, the helmsman would blow a loud whistle that hung from the binnacle rail at all times.

Sailing downwind and going for speed required constant attention to the spinnaker, frequent sail changes, and precise steering. Gone were the days when an ocean passage meant the relaxed meal, the catnap, the ritual sun sight, the good read. One of the biggest fears when flying spinnakers is the dreaded wrap—when it goes a bit wrong and gets itself caught around the forestay. This can be a nightmare at sea and in extreme cases can require a trip aloft to sort out the problem. Happily, there is a solution, and the single most useful device on our fast passage was the spinnaker net that we manufactured in Las Palmas. The net is hoisted like a staysail, and is sail-shaped and usually made of strips of webbing. It prevents a collapsing spinnaker from crossing inside the forestay and wrapping around the forestay in light air. This doesn't really affect the airflow to the spinnaker and can also serve as a gybe guide.

It was hard work. In three weeks I lost 18 pounds—I recommend the diet. But then there was the satisfaction of going fast, and being in the lead. That was the intangible. We were also the *enfants terribles*, as we pushed the boat past other boats, over-canvassed, changing spinnakers day and night—a practice that earned us the reputation of vampire pirates in the fleet. We often used a storm spinnaker in strong winds, a sail that had been commissioned by *Pirate*'s first owner years before, and which gave us good advantage. We baptized it "The Whomper," after the film *Winds*.

I had originally planned to take *Pirate* on a southerly route, below the 20th parallel. All sailing directions counseled me to follow the old orders of the British Admiralty: "South till the butter melts, then west." Yet the weather patterns over the North Atlantic in the fall of 1992 dictated otherwise. With regularly updated information from Bob Rice in Massachusetts, and using the strategy of our Australian navigator Simon Wynn, we sailed west from Gomera in the Canaries, and stayed above the 25th parallel until midway, at 045°W, and only then did we dip a bit south, arriving just below the 24th parallel on Thanksgiving Day. From there on we kept west pretty much along the 24th parallel until landfall. The basic reason was that the Azores High had been pushed to 40°N, 059'W by November 20. This allowed a series of lows to push their way north, and enabled us to sail on their edge, closer to Columbus' original route than we had planned. Without knowing it, Columbus followed the great circle route between the

Canaries and San Salvador, which put him slightly north of the 27th parallel during the longest part of his passage until he went south, ten days before his landfall.

As a schoolboy with an interest in weather, I had learned that the wind direction is oriented along the isobars, and that wind speed is greater as the isobars get closer together. The surface wind direction generally toes-in about 15 degrees towards the center of the lows and away from the center of the highs. This is due to surface friction. For a given distance between isobars, wind speeds will be greater around curved sets than along straight ones. Some of the synoptic charts, especially the English ones, will have a scale in the corner of the chart to convert the distance between isobars at a particular latitude into wind speed. This basic knowledge, and Bob Rice's advice, helped us a great deal. The centers of the highs, as well as the centers of the lows, have little or no wind. Other areas of calm are high-pressure ridgelines and "cols," the region between the lows moving side by side. On charts, I learned that surface analyses are the best. I also learned that nephanalysis (the analysis of cloud forms) over a charted area would indicate the location of pressure systems. On my first crossing, going east, I appreciated the usefulness of Gulf Stream Analysis from NOAA, and the limited usefulness of sea ice analysis, for there is no way to track icebergs. I knew enough to feel confident that the forecast by a local meteorologist in Las Palmas, proffered during the skippers' meeting, was based on 500 MB analyses from the local airport. They contradicted the surface analyses I had received from Bob Rice. What to do? At the skippers' meeting we were told "light air; go south." Instead I knew we would have a cold front over us at the starting line, with a strong breeze. That is exactly what happened. We did not follow the fleet around the northern tip of Gran Canaria, and gained an advantage as a result.

En route to the New World, the tradewinds never showed up, yet we had enough wind (and a more efficient sail plan) to better Columbus' crossing by 12 days. We saw northerlies during the first three days, then southerlies that eased and wasted as they pleased during the following week, then something resembling the easterly trades for five consecutive days, then southerlies again, then light and variable winds, with line squalls until we crossed the finish line. By and large the winds kept an easterly component and a good speed.

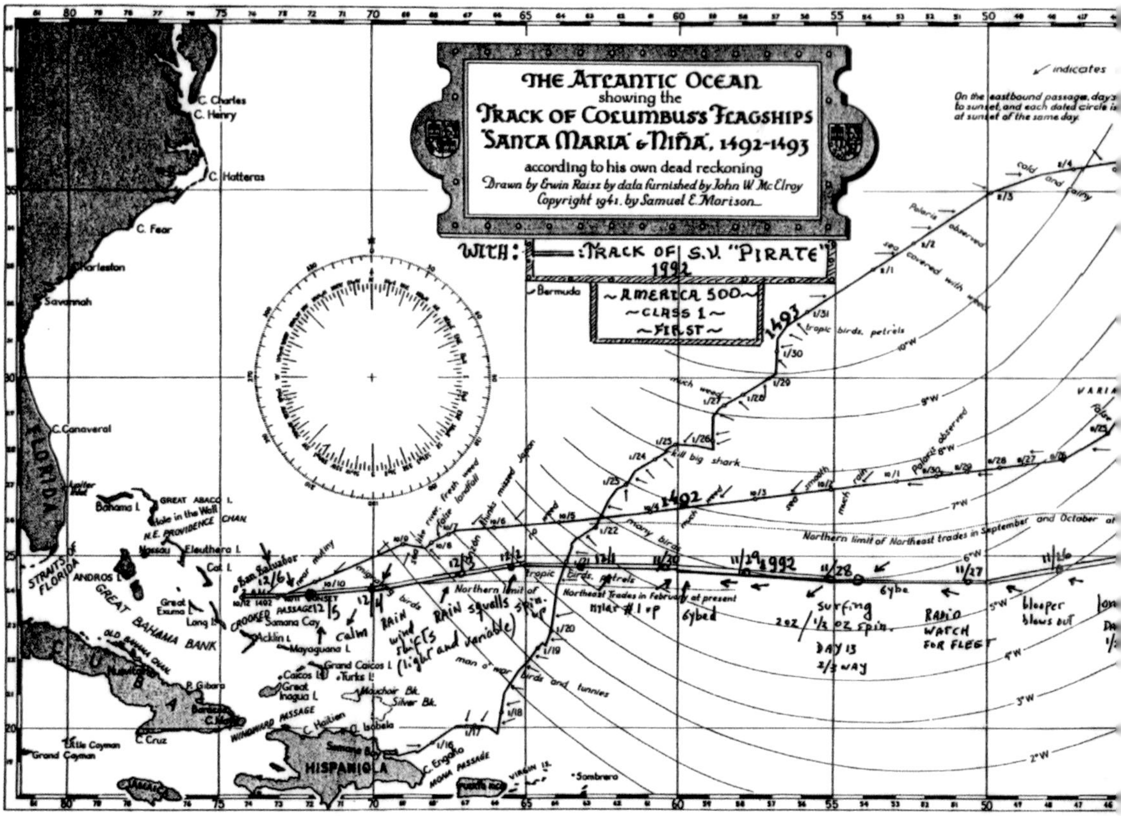

Chart Of Columbus and the America 500.

During the first two-thirds of the passage we achieved daily runs of 180 miles and better, broad reaching in 20 knots of breeze and more, with occasional bursts of 27–30 knots. *Pirate*'s old 2 oz. Dacron chute (The Whomper), and a new medium-air spinnaker, colored blood-red with the Venetian Lion of St. Mark in gold in the middle, served us well. I do not know what is more demanding: changing spinnakers in the middle of the night, or steering under them in the dark. But we were "vampire pirates" because we never doused the spinnakers at night, and managed it well, under the supervision of our Greek taskmaster, Manolis Pantelis. Only occasionally did we hoist the Mylar #1, the nylon drifter, or the staysail. Most of the time we used a heavy "storm" spinnaker to carry us forward. Once, to stop the rolling, we had the blooper up as well, but in general we relied on flatter, reaching kites. The new loose-footed mainsail from Hong Kong was a pleasure to trim.

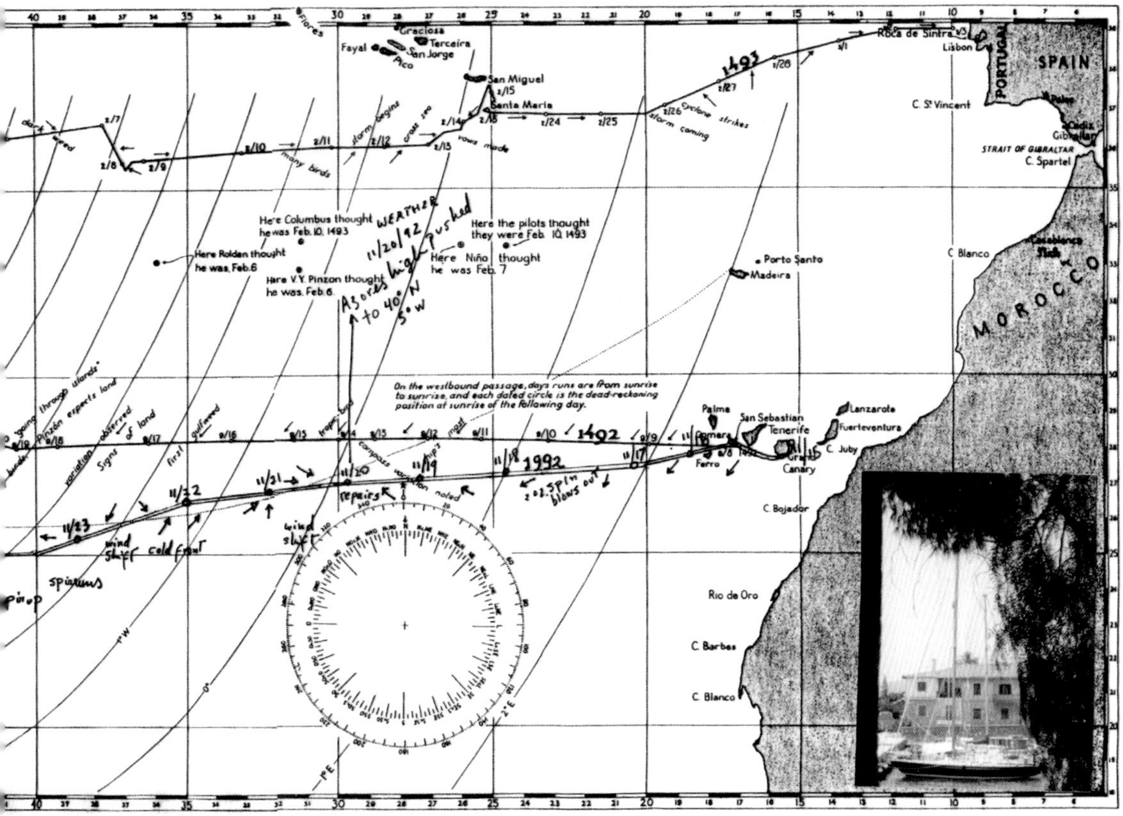

Our life on board—five men cooped up in a diminutive space for three full weeks—was anything but leisurely. Living conditions were made harsh by our determination to keep top level performance. There was little distraction from the ship's constant chores, with the exception of the culinary feats of our sailor chef, Bro Uttal. He managed to produce a festival of ethnic foods: pita bread baked on board encased genuine falafel. A rock-hard bread from Crete named *paximadia* (Παξιμάδια), and similar to the ancient Puglian *freselle*, softened by water and oil accompanied feta cheese and calamata olives as an hors d'oeuvre. Pepperoni pizzas emerged sizzling from the galley. Portuguese recipes for dried cod tickled the palate. And the feast went on: a string of edible treats begotten by an unholy alliance between Barbarossa and Julia Child.

The changing environment and the necessity to keep speed up make racing across an ocean very different from cruising across an ocean. A cruising yacht threatened by bad weather will shorten sail; racers seldom allow themselves this option until it is unsafe. While racing, light air is as demanding as heavy weather.

We tried numerous tricks to squeeze that fraction of a knot that, over a period of time, makes the difference between winning and losing. We were always on alert. When the weather turned, we sensed it. Subtle signs announce the approach of a squall: a sullen oily swell, a brassy sky. The barometer drops—or not. Heavy clouds pile in the sky. Rain comes, and then stops. The squall is not yet in sight but those signs, and a dog-like instinct, are enough. It is best to act on first impulse, for there is no time for second thoughts. Change foresails, or furl them. Change spinnakers; reef the main. And then, change sails quickly again, if the squall does not materialize, lest we lose precious time.

In this race we were lucky to have with us a first-rate mate and tactician, and one of the world's finest all-around sailors, Manolis Pantelis. Sailmaker, skipper, designer, rigger, Manolis had been around ocean racing, and racing around the buoys for over 30 years. He held desk navigation in contempt, and put more faith in his ability to gauge the smell of the wind, decipher the language of the clouds, and interpret the changing color of the water than in using instruments and calculations as a guide.

Pirate performed admirably, despite her age and weight, and stayed well ahead of even larger boats. Like all the other Swans, *Pirate* lived up to the reputation of the Nautor yard. *Pirate* was the smallest, and the only black Swan; the others were all white. In the racing fleet, there was one ultra-light-displacement boat, *Niob 6,* a forerunner of today's fastest boats. In my days, boats carved their way through the water. Only a great increase in the driving force could enable the vessel to climb up and over her own bow wave and escape the hull-speed limit by planing. Planing and surfing are episodic, not sustained. The maximum potential speed through the water is predictable: theoretical hull speed is about one and a quarter times the square root of the waterline length in feet. None of these relationships are valid once new designs and materials make sustained planing possible, which started with ULDBs and culminates with the use of foils.

It is now possible to cross oceans on giant sleds at the speed of surfing boards.

Manolis Pantelis, sailmaker, designer, rigger

They require great stamina and skill, but the day will come when even retired couples will cross large bodies of water at double the speed of their predecessors, with the same or more amenities, greater safety, and greater ease of handling than our older heavier boats. Perhaps we will see older couples on high-tech speedsters roaming the deep blue, such as the Baltic 142' sloop named *Canova* launched in 2019.

The facts of nautical life and its great diversity make handicapping the only solution when racing boats are of different sizes and designs. For the America 500, the system used was the British Channel Handicap. The yachts were grouped into two separate divisions, Racing and Cruising, and further subdivided into classes. There were exceptions however, and allowances were made for the cruisers to use engines. In the end, the rally organizers used a rating system of their own concoction, which led some participants to suspect a culinary conclusion for the overall results. Were they cooked? We shall never know. For us, the journey was more about people than about rules.

On more than one occasion, the journey bore witness to the best traditions of seamanship in terms of assistance in emergencies and need. A Canadian boat was halfway across the Atlantic when one of the crew was thrown across the galley into the navigation station (a common and dangerous occurrence) and sustained a painful rib injury. The next day a French boat racing from Casablanca to Guadeloupe was alerted by radio. They approached the vessel in distress. A veterinarian aboard that vessel jumped overboard and was retrieved by the Lifesling of the boat in need. After diagnosing and dressing the injury, in consultation with a hospital in Guadeloupe, he administered medication and returned to his boat, again retrieved with the help of the Lifesling. It was a story of gallantry and good seamanship with a happy end.

During the first two weeks of the passage, our 19-year-old 38-footer managed to stay not far behind a more modern Swan 46 and a Whitbread Race (an around-the-world race, which has been superseded by today's Volvo Ocean Race) maxi, and ahead of a BOC 60-footer. We did fall behind Jacques Pelletier's 46 LDB (light displacement boat), which reportedly surfed on occasions at 25 knots, and *Adix*, the 211-foot three-masted schooner that took line honors.

After three arduous weeks came landfall. On the last few days of the race, very light and variable winds lost us some of the advantage, yet we were the 25th boat to cross the finish line in San Salvador, the first in both elapsed and corrected time in our class, and the fourth overall on corrected time. Citing safety reasons, the race organizers decided to close the finish line at dusk and reopen it at dawn, which gave an unfair advantage to the laggards and penalized the leading boats. The crews of the forward boats did not receive this well. We felt that *Pirate* had ruled the waves while the organizers had waved the rules. But the bad feeling was soon forgotten in the festivities that followed.

The 110 finishers arrived singly or in small groups.The Finnish yachts crossed the finish line almost in formation, at dawn on December 6, which is Finland's Independence Day. Like Nelson at Trafalgar, *Pirate* drove a wedge in their formation, and crossed a few seconds behind the leading Finnish boat. Most of the boats made their symbolic arrival in San Salvador, called Guanahani by the natives, and then quickly headed towards Georgetown to await the awards ceremony on December 19. For *Pirate*, next was a short-handed sail back to the US, via Nassau and the Berry Islands. Manolis was my mate: it was his first visit to America. *Pirate*'s crew returned to the places they lived, and were all left with the unforgettable sense of having accomplished something special. There is something about an ocean passage that charges the soul—we do it because, as Sir Francis Chichester said, "it intensifies life."

After the transatlantic rally, I returned to teach at New York University. Before setting sail, many friends and colleagues from the Dean of the Faculty to my students, had endorsed my resolution with great sympathy. Others, however, thought it was incorrect to join in the celebration of what to them was the first act of genocide. This is a standard "politically correct" view. Here I'd like to set them straight.

Columbus has been judged harshly and unfairly with the standards of our age. That is bad enough, and it stems from the Western habit of considering the past as riddled with malice. I blame Western philosophers for this, those Europeans who thought that the anatomy of man is a key to the anatomy of the ape—a story with an uplifting meaning through and through, as if the intimations of "higher development" among the subordinate animal species and benighted previous generations can be understood only after "the higher development" is already known.

We should not take the evolutionary and moral high horse. I am a modest Darwinian instead: we are the result of a series of accidents that started with an ape: a jumpy descent with modifications, which, by the way, may not end well. But the revisionist history to which Columbus' figure has been subjected—and which, some think, should forbid celebration—is mistaken on the facts.

Columbus never sought to discover a new continent, and never thought that his arrival in what we call the Bahamas was the spearhead of an invasion, or that it would open the enormous possibilities for rape, pillage, epidemic disease, slavery, and forceful settlement that would ensue. He wanted to arrive to a known place by different means. His motive was commercial not colonial, and religion followed suit, as befitted a Genovese adventurer at the end of the middle ages. Hence his statement that will seem puzzling to revisionists, with which I have opened this chapter: "It is easy to discover what another has discovered before." Columbus thought he had landed in the vicinity of Cipango, or Japan, and that the first island he saw was a gateway to China. He believed correctly that the earth was round, but calculated the distances incorrectly. As Admiral Morison wrote, Columbus figured the Indies were just 68° west of the Canary Islands. Calculated travel *distance:* 3080 NM. *Actual distance from* Tenerife to Jakarta: 7313 NM. Margin of error: 58 percent. He stumbled upon what we call the Americas on his way.

Going around a relatively small globe was *not* a fifteenth century prelude to Star Trek—the open road of discovery, the restless search of novelty, and in it, of one's destiny. Instead, in Columbus' words, "*el mundo es poca cosa*," there isn't much to the world. What did he mean by that?

There is a straightforward explanation. When the Ottoman Turks closed the commercial route to the Orient by land, Columbus and others searched another way: go east by sailing west. If the Hellespont was closed, they chose the other gate, western gate: the Pillars of Hercules. Above all, Columbus' was a great feat of seamanship. He not only got there *but came back* as well.

There may be however another interpretation. It is as if Columbus had been convinced that no principle of causality could determine the outcome of a story, whether positive or negative, and therefore, in the absence of a story, there could be no real *novitas*. In 17 days away from any sight of shore, I was in the throes of this hallucination. As we followed Columbus' route 500 years after him, I had the disquieting sense that three small caravels were still sailing on the surface of a Moebius strip. As happens always when going offshore, space and time join and disappear in the shape of a perpetual horizon. Had we embarked aboard *Pirate* on an endless voyage of mystery? To pursue this account further would mean leaving common narrative and entering the magic world of Jorge Luis Borges.

Landfall in the Bahamas with red spinnaker. Photo credit: Simon Wynn

Recollections

An Ode to *Pirate*

By Bro Uttal

Sing, goddess, the glories of Pirate, *her races and voyages, her captain and her crews!*
Conceived with brilliance in New York by S&S, sprung forth from Nautor,
Pietarsaari's pride,
Fortunate in her devoted masters—though never moreso than with Juan Corradi—
To her crews, both curvetting filly and stout-timbered home upon the sea,
Darling of wind and wave, of Aeolus and Poseidon,
A creature of breath-stopping beauty and fierce, imposing purpose:
Black-hulled, tall-masted, flush-decked, straight-sheered, strong and fleet,
Worthy successor to the swift black hulls of the Achaeans,
Who beached on Ilium's pebbled shore and burnt the topless towers.

Of Pirate's *races and her victories, O goddess, sing the heart-lifting paean!*
In 1990, Newport to Bermuda, with Juan's far-sighted cunning,
With the calculations of Sid White, Nestor of navigators,
With Simon Wynn, eager tactician, recruiter of foredeck hands,
Pirate *plied West of the rhumb line favored by the ever-tacking fleet,*
Seeking the eddies that would speed her way, seeking the filling of the
Southwest wind.
The wind eluded her; she tacked to find it; when finally it breathed,
She tacked once more—the last of only three!—and reached straight for
St. David's light.
The favor of the gods, the skill of men, and blind beginner's luck
Brought her silver enough to dazzle Bermuda's fabled privateers:
Not one, or two, or three, or even four, but five great trophies bear the name
of Pirate,
Multiple winner of that storied race.

And what of 1992, in the Atlantic 500, half rally, half race,
Marking the quincentennial of Colombo's quest for Eastern silks and spices,
First of his voyages, a discovery by mistake, a world-changer?
Sing, goddess, not just of Juan and Simon (navigator then), but of Manolis Pantelis:
Odysseus come again, the wine-dark Aegean coursing through his veins,
Sorcerer of spinnakers, reputed Vampire for creeping up the fleet at night,
When others all had doused their 'chutes for fear of wraps.
Manolis the Sailing Master, coach of Olympians, wily and wild -
He it was devised the staysail wrap-preventer, that net of fabric tapes,
The trick that empowered Pirate, *flying her spinnakers always,*
Parting the gray Atlantic, surging down billows, scattering spume,
Swiftly to raise San Salvador, her crew going ashore to kiss the earth,
as doubtless had Colombo.
Yes, First in Class—but that was little next to the wonder of changing-color dawns
in mid-Atlantic,
Little next to the sight of her parading among the Bahamas,
Led by her blood-red 'chute bearing the golden Lion of St. Mark, patron of Venice
(from whence the forebears of Annika Barbarigos, co-adjutor of Pirate*'s acquisition,*
Had sent their galleys into the Aegean—warlike merchants, building the Stato
da Mar).

From Marblehead to Halifax, in 1997, no laurels crowned the black swan's prow.
She was not made for mediocre winds, for hunting lifts, edging away from lulls.
The foredeck did their best, also the afterguard: Herr Forster at the charts,
Scanning weather and wind and sea state, current and tide, plotting and plotting
again, eking out the least advantage.
Bob Stewart, handler of ships, master of massive diesels, stood stoic at the wheel,
impervious to all frustration.
Relief came from the galley, a cornucopia of dishes geared to each ethnicity:
Hispanic bacalao, and lentils with morcilla; Teutonic sauerbraten, also herrings; beef stew
for the Celts; stone-baked pizzas, savory pastas—Italianate, yet universal fare.

Once more ashore, with loved ones close at hand, gloom turned to revelry:
Delightful Gallic dishes in the town, and at the Captain's Dinner, a feast of lobsters, scallops, mussels by the score
(One member of the crew banned from the buffet, guilty of Gargantuan appetite).
And then, of course, the ceremonial photo:
Pirates all, sporting their eyepatches, brandishing cutlasses, grinning from ear to ear, growling a chorus of "Arrgh!"

Sing, goddess, of Pirate*'s many races and long passages,*
Shuttling between New World and Old,
From Santorini to Newport, once more to the Bermuda race,
To Scottish isles, to North Sea and Baltic, to the rock-strewn Bothnian Gulf.

And sing you ever of Pirate*'s grace and power, her beauty and strength;*
Of the valor and camaraderie of those who sailed her;
Of the transporting joy she gave us all.

* * *

BRO UTTAL is a researcher, writer, and editor who has served on the Board of Editors at *Fortune* magazine and as Senior Research Consultant at McKinsey & Co. Along with (the fictional) Major Tickeridge of the Royal Corps of Halberdiers, Bro believes that, "Any damn fool can make himself *un*comfortable," whether in the field or at sea. And knowing how an interesting variety of hot meals can support morale, he became one of Pirate's most enterprising cooks. Today he cruises the waters of Long Island Sound and points Northeast, as well as in Greece, the Saronic Gulf and points South. (An oenophile, he also holds the title of *Cavaliere del Sovrano e Nobilissimo Ordine dello Antico Recioto della Valpolicella.*)

7

FROM THE APENNINES TO THE TROPICS

I really don't know why it is that all of us
are so committed to the sea, except I think it's because
in addition to the fact that the sea changes,
and the light changes, and ships change,
it's because we all came from the sea.

—JOHN F. KENNEDY

In the year 1998, I took a long leave from academic and administrative duties at Washington Square to oversee the restoration of a famed palace in Florence—at the time the premier site of NYU abroad. In that magnificent city, my wife and I designed the curriculum and academic program of the university.

I found out that Florence was all about preservation and that New York was all about development. The marriage of those two was not made in heaven, and could not have lasted long. Occasional collusion and reciprocal corruption—above my head and behind my back—formed not a solid bond. And there I was, acting as an honest broker. What a foolish thing to do!

For two years, I was the executive director of New York University in Florence, and the fake lord of La Pietra, a Renaissance villa with 60 rooms,

Our home in Florence: the Gilded Cage of Villa La Pietra

172 statues, and thousands of works of art ranging from the sublime to the silly. It was graced by acres of splendid gardens and olive groves in the ingrate city of Dante. Its last real lord was Sir Harold Acton, the great Anglo-Florentine aesthete.

But all this, which I have just described with savage brevity, was of the least importance. What mattered was the entry ticket to a world of exquisite refinement, with echoes of a glorious past. Florence taught me the meaning of elegance, and of the *bella figura.*

Being an actor on the stage all the time can be asphyxiating. As J.L. Borges wrote, it is everything and nothing. My part was *il direttore*—a notable of Florence. To escape such a gilded cage in a city that is a fish bowl, one must have either a secret vice or an outdoor passion. Christina and I had *Pirate*, our magic carpet, docked in a marina in Liguria, and ready to carry us off. The rather posh marina and shipyard of Porto Lotti

The Director of Villa La Pietra

was situated on the outskirts of La Spezia on the eastern side of the Gulf of La Spezia. Today it provides over 500 berths for yachts up to 80 meters on three long pontoons and two breakwater quays, plus a host of additional services, some of them delightful.

In the days of whaling ships, two voyages were considered sufficient to qualify a future master for command, in which time he learned from experience, and from examples, all that was needed. In the twelve years we had owned *Pirate*, we never relinquished her command, but had nonetheless much to learn from the ship herself, and from sailing mates with greater skill and experience than ourselves. Some 20,000 miles later, we trusted we had somehow earned our ship's respect.

For two years, she was moored in La Spezia, while we held our jobs in Florence. During this period, we drove from Florence to the Ligurian marina on weekends from April through September, and cruised the Med during our month-long vacations in

June. Much as we love the little towns in Cinque Terre, the fact remains that the Ligurian Sea suffers in the summer from the general Mediterranean fate. Most days there is little or no wind (only gentle shore breezes at night will drive a boat from port to port along the Italian coast). When the wind finally comes, it generally blows a gale, born in the Gulf of Lyon, which gathers strength if there is a secondary low in Northern Liguria, and unloads its fury on the shores of Corsica and Sardinia. Winds of 50 knots and a nasty chop, even under deep blue skies, are no one's idea of fun. An exception to this pattern is the occasional *sirocco*, a sickly wind from the south, which brings red sand from the African desert and drives some people, as mentioned earlier, to murderous excess. Our summer vacations were spent at sea, cruising Corsica, Sardinia, and the Balearic Isles, having for company each other, our springer spaniel, Bonaparte, and occasional guests.

We visited magnificent towns and coves, had great food and great fun, but in terms of seamanship, we practiced the standard art of Mediterranean cruising: motoring between gales.

As the new millennium dawned, I had had enough of NYU's uncouth and Florentine intrigues. I resigned my position, leaving a good job and some good works behind. We wished to get out of the arbors and ardors of Acton Hall, and into the open sea.

In June of 2000, Christina and I aboard *Pirate* left the shores of Italy for good. A steady breeze carried us from La Spezia to Calvi, an old town in the northwest corner of Corsica, where Napoleon's father was born, and a welcoming port of call for westbound boats. From Calvi we sailed to a favorite harbor, Mahon in Minorca (one of the few true fjords in the Mediterranean and an old hideout for the British fleet), and then set a course for the Bay of Palma. We stayed for three weeks at the Real Club Náutico of Palma de Mallorca, engrossed in several repair and upgrade projects in one of the best nautical service centers in the world, and one of the most elegant old cities in Europe.

Our stop in the small island of Formentera was meant to be a short visit to a quaint time warp: nudist beaches, California-style bars, superannuated hippies, new age tourists, high tan and low amperage, and, luckily, one Internet café. But after

Juan and Bonaparte In Gibraltar.

twelve years, our gearbox quit. It was examined and replaced, while we sat in port and waited patiently for parts. Three weeks later we were able to sail to mainland Spain. We hopped from port to port in high season—all crowded, requiring reservations at marinas which have become shopping malls attached to Potemkin villages, to service Arab yuppies, German retirees, British middle managers, and the occasional Spaniard—all the way to Gibraltar.

The Mediterranean shores of Spain seem to have exiled the guitar, banned the scent of jasmine and the taste of manzanilla, to welcome instead the throbbing sounds of disco and the munching of fast food. But the nonsense is skin-deep. If you speak the language, you may soon engage in interesting conversation, savoring the quick wit and the funny turn of phrase that has spiced Spanish talk since the days of Cervantes and Quevedo. And if you still insist on jasmine, guitar, and manzanilla, all you have to do is sail through the Straits of Gibraltar and dock at Cadiz or Seville (50 miles up the Guadalquivir River), visit the ports of Rota, Chipiona, Santa Maria or San Lucar de Barrameda, to see perennial Spain displayed: love and gore, passion and faith, beauty and cruelty entwined, the same people who gave a new world to the old.

But first you must pass the great turnstile of the sea, the ancient Pillars of Hercules: Mount Hecla in Morocco and the Rock of Gibraltar, a Jurassic appendix to the continent of Europe. Between these two pillars (only eight miles apart at the narrowest point) flow the largest volume of traffic, the most capricious currents, and some of the most savage bursts of air on the planet. For a number of reasons, it is much easier to enter the Mediterranean Sea through this gate than to exit into the Atlantic; although the tide moves in two directions, the current flow is always into the Mediterranean. Bound westward, a vessel must wait for a weather window and the right tide, and even then, play with several other variables. The wind has to be easterly, but not gale force, when reaching the other end of the funnel, and the movement of the tide must be gauged in terms of the estimated course and speed of the vessel. Within the general tide flow, one must ride the favorable, and avoid the contrary, streams. These shift all the time, and the tides sometimes fail to move on schedule, mindless of the tables. If you get it wrong, you will find yourself going backwards! If you make progress, but the wind is against the tide, you are in for a wild ride. If wind, tide, and current are well disposed, you may still run out of time, with only four hours of good sailing before heading into a foul current.

August arrived. *Pirate* needed work and new parts in Gibraltar, including new mounts and a lift pump for the engine, a SSB radio for communications offshore, a satellite emergency beacon for safety, some charts for the Canaries, the Cape Verdes, and the Caribbean. While we supplied the ship and waited for the wind to shift to the east, we got acquainted with the town, its history, its gardens, and the unique mixture of Gibraltar-born Spaniards, British expatriates, Indian merchants, and their faiths: Catholic, Presbyterian, Muslim, and the Judaism of Ladino-speaking Sephardim. After two weeks we left the Rock, somewhat poorer, well-rested, and shipshape.

We sailed away one afternoon under a decent weather window. We zigged and zagged over the tidal streams. We overcame a moment of foul current. By nightfall we cleared the Straits off Cape Trafalgar. The ghosts of Nelson and of Patrick O'Brian made themselves felt in these shallow waters, now riddled with fishing nets and traps. At dawn we approached the Bay of Cadiz and sailed into the port of Rota, under a freshening breeze. These were familiar waters, and the approaches are straightforward, if you keep an eye on the rocks off Cadiz and on the reefs and shallows near Rota. The American Naval Base lies one mile to the east, with large transport ships anchored in the roadstead. Even inside the breakwater, one feels the difference from the Med: at spring tides, the floating pontoons go up and down twelve feet! Rota has a modern and pleasant marina next to an interesting old town. Thus summer came to an end.

We felt that our boat was safe in Rota, tucked in port for two months, under the care of the same team that had worked on her eight years before, on the occasion of the America 500 Transatlantic Race. Meanwhile, we had other business waiting in New York—chores quite remote from the affairs of the sea. Eight weeks passed before we felt ready to return. When we did, we found our ship in good repair: a fresh coat of bottom paint, new running rigging, seacocks, winches, all inspected and clean, tanks and battery banks full to the brim. The town and the marina were bare and cold. The first autumn gales had already battered the port; the days were short. *Pirate*'s new crew began to assemble on board, five in all, three old *Pirate* hands, two new hands. We studied the weather (a fresh breeze from the ENE) and set a rhumb line course for Madeira, allowing for the south-going current outside the bay. Even in the late fall, it is possible to lay the course for Madeira without problem, though westerly winds blow with greater frequency.

We left Rota on November 10, propelled by a weakening *levanter*, the easterly wind from the Straits; it had reached gale force in Gibraltar but blew itself out in two days. The ensuing calm forced us to motor for 18 hours, until the wind returned, this time from the west, as we feared. In order to avoid headwinds and delays, we decided not to go to Madeira and Porto Santo (visited in 1992), and made a more southerly course instead. We carried a fuller set of the sails, directly to the Canaries, and fished all the way—iridescent *mahi mahi* and tuna abound in these waters. We sighted the island of Lanzarote the morning of November 15. By midday, we were tied to a pontoon in Puerto Calero, one of the neatest marinas in that part of the world, and a good base to explore the strange volcanic island. The cones of Timanfaya, barren mountains of fire, some hot and fuming, bring forth desolate images from Dante and somber sounds from Wagner.

From Lanzarote we sailed to the neighboring island of Fuerteventura, once famous for its long and empty beaches but now a chaotic construction site for the tourist trade. We left the indifferent Puerto Castillo in that unfortunate isle towards the far more interesting Puerto de Mogan in the southwest corner of Gran Canaria. We arrived in Gran Canaria on November 19.

A sail to the Canaries for a boat bound for the Caribbean is usually a shakedown for the Atlantic crossing. The 700 miles separating mainland Spain from its Canarian possessions are a good test of the boat, her stores, and her crew. In our case, *Pirate* had the advantage of repeat performance, having followed this path before in 1992. But carrying new and untested crew members always entails a risk—bouts of seasickness and immaturity beset the newcomers—and we were scheduled to add a new "green" member in the Canaries, to replace *Pirate*'s long-standing navigator Simon Wynn, who had to return to his job.

The longer voyage across the pond was fraught with uncertainty. As it turned out, other signs, which ancient mariners would attribute to an overruling Providence, made it painfully obvious that a short-handed but happy ship is preferable to a crowded and tense boat. In late November, the trades had not yet settled, and the weather forecasts augured long days of motoring and weak variable winds. Upon leaving port, *Pirate* spoke in her own voice: her gearbox gave out again, prompting a more thorough inspection of the engine, the cutlass bearing, and the propeller pitch. In distant Buenos Aires, my father's long illness took a turn for the worse. We decided to abort the passage, disband the crew, and wait for a more propitious time. We would haul out, fix the boat, mend the soul, bid farewell to the crew, and fly to Argentina for a more important, definitive good-bye.

As in a sequence of prophesied and orchestrated trials, all such events took place—repairs, disillusion, dissolution, flight, reunion, death, mourning, and return—within the short span of one month. At the beginning of the year, we come back to our old boat. From Buenos Aires we brought a talisman to inspire us and cherish on the bulkhead: a watercolor of the little double-ender *Leg II* surfing in a strong southwest gale, near the Horn, painted by her skipper, the legendary solo sailor Vito Dumas. Brian Cardello, a good friend from New Hampshire, experienced sailor, and one-time racing crew on *Pirate* (in the Marblehead to Halifax Ocean Race) joined us this time. The three of us felt right, and everything fell into place. The repaired boat and her smaller, now compatible crew were finally released by fate, as if an invisible Will had given us our leave. Y2K passed. The true Millennium dawned. We sailed to the new world. Once again, we followed the old instructions of the English Navy when Britannia ruled the waves: "South till the butter melts; then West."

Everybody loves the tradewinds. We have all read accounts of fast passages under steady winds and friendly skies, with rhythmic swells and strings of puffy clouds (*cumulus humilis*), under the same sail configuration for days on end. Our crossing became almost a textbook case. We left port on January 3rd, dipping south first, below 20 degrees of latitude, and setting a course closer to the Cape Verde Islands than either the rhumb line or great circle would suggest (the difference between these courses on this passage is a negligible 17 miles); we indeed met the northeast trades. The north equatorial current of 1 to 1.5 knots helped us along, so that we attained an average of 155 miles a day. Our biggest 24-hour run was 181 NM, running before winds of 20 to 25 knots under single-reefed main, with the working jib poled out wing-on-wing. Our worst day's run was 138 NM. We averaged 6.4 knots for the distance to Grenada of 2,800 miles. Our actual sailing distance was closer to 3,000 miles since we gybed downwind. Near the Cape Verde's, we were disturbed by cross seas and a big, wretched northwest swell, no doubt the residue of the tremendous January gales in the upper North Atlantic. Closer to the Caribbean we encountered squalls after sunset. Traffic was scant, and signs of marine life, few: three large ships, sunbathing turtles, one right whale, schools of dolphins, many flying fish, and, closer to land, the birds (Bermuda Longtails, gannets, frigate birds). Contrary to northern lore, red skies in the morning announce splendid days in the tropics. The last 300 miles became a sleigh ride, past Barbados and into the Grenada Channel. We did it in 19 days.

The boat was properly canvassed most of the time. We did not want to break anything, or risk harm to the rig and crew. The one time we disregarded this caution we regretted it, as *Pirate* dipped her bow while surfing down 15-foot waves. Running downwind in these conditions, the wind vane cannot be trusted (as it can be when sailing under double headsails and no mainsail) to avoid an accidental gybe especially if a rogue wave distracts the vessel from her course. A strong preventer is essential. Most of the time we steered by hand. We kept single watches of three hours each. If there was reason to expect convection squalls, especially at night, we reduced the watches to two hours. Being three and in good physical shape, the system gave us plenty of rest. Many of the cruising boats are crewed by couples; we kept in touch with a 35-foot Hallberg-Rassy sloop some 200 miles behind us, by radio, twice a day. The young Swiss couple in this case kept a simple, but fatiguing watch: Jean-Claude would keep watch and/or steer during the night, Graziella would cook and keep watch during most of the day. They sometimes made music together—he on the accordion, she on the flute. We became friends, and once we were in Grenada, spent some days together exploring the rainforest and harvesting nutmeg.

We enjoyed delicious meals; fresh pizzas, and freshly baked bread, were our favorites. Plenty of water, some beer, juices, and a glass of wine at night, helped us keep the cheer. Fresh fruit (citrus, apples, and the versatile kiwi) lasted us all the way. The small blue-fin tuna we caught one afternoon gave us *sushi* treats, and steaks, for a good three days. Pasta, rice, couscous, curries of all sorts, and lentil soup were all consumed with gusto. Spanish cans of saucy octopus and squid were a big hit. Vegetables, cabbage, and all manner of tubers and roots kept well. Unrefrigerated eggs lasted a month, turned once a day. The fridge and watermaker worked like a charm. We turned them on only a few hours a day. Running the engine for a mere three hours kept the batteries happy, which in turn fed our simple electric needs. We burned only 12 gallons of fuel in 19 days (replacing the injector nozzles paid off in a big way). The biggest guzzlers were, predictably, the desalinator and the transmission blasts of the offshore radio.

Our chef was also the chief communications officer, and deftly handled "the net." In addition to the official forecasts, and the paid services of Commanders' Weather, several amateur nets transmitted useful weather information for different parts of the Atlantic Ocean. To us, the most crucial was Herb's Net. Herb Hilgenberg (he was more commonly known as *Southbound II*) should have been canonized. He broadcast from Ontario on 12359kHz from 2000 UTC (universal time). Herb gave a detailed forecast to each boat that contacted him, and plenty of accurate advice. Just listening to his communications with other vessels gave us a very useful picture of weather systems across vast swaths of the sea. Herb forged a community where we followed the adventures of fellow sailors. By the end of the passage, we considered Herb a trusted friend. The French Maritime Mobile Net also helped route our Swiss friends in tandem, aboard *Manatee,* the Hallberg Rassy 35. Daniel, their router in Paris, put *Pirate* on his screen, suggesting waypoints and tactics. Herb and Daniel generally concurred, and we were all the happier for it.

The last day at sea we sailed under mainsail alone. We had to slow the boat to make landfall in daylight, as the approaches to Prickly Bay in Grenada are studded with nasty sunken rocks. In mid-morning we docked the boat in a charming small marina where fresh green lawns were dotted with palm trees. It has an atmosphere reminiscent of an old Humphrey Bogart film. On the hard, overlooking the bay, our old black Swan enjoyed a well-deserved and pampered rest, not far from *Velsheda,* a majestic J-class sloop from the 30's.

Pirate remained in Grenada for a full year, based in Prickly Bay, a friendly and laid back marina with haulout facilities and helpful locals, who watched the boat, especially Sam Mangealoo, the aging dean of ladies' men on the island—a delightful fellow and our best insurance policy. During our stay we sailed the Grenadines and the Lesser Antilles, and enjoyed the good winter weather and the trades. We then took the yacht to Antigua, where she had a gracious host and keeper—the honorary Italian consul and great sailor, Carlo Falcone.

Finally, in 2002, we undertook the long trip back to home waters in Narragansett Bay, via Bermuda, and arrived in Newport on July 4, to be greeted by a jittery Coast Guard, heavily armed and obviously on guard after the 9/11 attack. Home, to a nervous homeland, at last.

8

It's Only Water: Let's Do It Again

They that go down to the sea in ships,
that do business in great waters;
these see the works of the Lord,
and His wonders in the deep.

—PSALMS, 107: 23-30, KJV

Plain Facts

We wished to go far and wide, and mostly north. Why north? The term is shifting and elusive: there is always a "north" from where one stands (except on the North Pole). But the North we had in mind is the North full of symbols and poetry that evokes a passionate response in most people, especially sailors. The idea of North holds the promise of purification, an escape from the limits of civilized life. The way North is the way into the unknown.

It took six summers, each full of discovery, adventure, and camaraderie—a feat not easily accomplished when five or six humans live in close proximity surrounded by the unknown. At the end of this northern saga we let our beloved vessel go, with the assurance that after all those miles she was coming back to seas that she could call home.

LOG RECOLLECTIONS

What follows is a summary of our adventures, culled from the logbooks of *Pirate*, with the names of the crews that made it possible, in the Atlantic, the North Sea, and the Baltic Sea from 2004 until 2010.

1. North Atlantic Crossing
2. Irish Sea
3. North Sea
4. Baltic
5. Sea of Aland
6. The Canals of Sweden
7. Skagerrak
8. Kateggat
9. Denmark
10. Spain

Leg	Distance in NM	Year
Bermuda to Azores non-stop	1,960	2004
Cruising in the Azores	210	
Azores to Crosshaven, Cork (Ireland) non-stop	1,205	
Crosshaven to Dublin, then Belfast		
Belfast to Port Ellen (Scotland), then Oban		
Cruising the Inner Hebrides with the Single Malt Cruise	700	2005
Caledonian Canal to Inverness		
Inverness to Orkneys		
Orkney to Fair Isle		
Fair Isle to Shetland Islands		
Lerwick (Shetland) to Bergen (Norway)	40	2006
Bergen to Bodø (North of the Arctic Circle)		
Cruising the Old Islands and Back to Bodø	876	2007

Cruising Bodø and Saltenfjord to Rognan (Norway)	120	2008
Land transport of the yacht from Rognan (Norway) Through North Sweden and Lapland to Kokkola (Finland)	621	2008
North Finland to High Coast of Sweden to Oregrund Cruise of the Aland Islands West Coast of Finland from Nystad to Kokkola	900	2009
Kokkola/Peteresaari (Finland) to High Coast of Sweden, to Stockholm archipelago. Göta Canal to Gotenburg (Sweden) Gotenburg to Friedrikstad in Oslo Fjord (Norway) West Coast of Sweden Skagerrak and Kattegat to Kalundborg (Denmark)	1,510	2010
Transport by Ship from Kalundborg (DK) to Mallorca		
Total Miles in the Years 2004-2010	**Approx. 8500**	

I was skipper in each and all legs with Christina Spellman as first mate.

Friends and some members of the New York Yacht Club joined us for one or more legs of this cruise. We were:

Bruno Bruni
Paolo Bruni
Lauretta Bruno
Juan Corradi
Daniel Ebin
Robert Ebin
Gary Forster
Lily Louis
Robert Machesney
Peter Mahr
Dan Mayer
Fernando Oliveira
Manuel Oliveira
Tig Smith
Christina Spellman
Beth Steggall
Philip Steggall
Robert N. Stewart
Elizabeth Taylor

The Transatlantic Cruising leg of 2004.
Conquering the demons of an inauspicious start.

In June 2004, the Swan 38 *Pirate* celebrated her 30th Birthday, and for the fifth time in her life, she raced to Bermuda. As the first yacht to cross the starting line in Class 1, she had the privilege of leading the entire fleet of 157 boats in their quest of the St. David's Lighthouse Trophy. But races are about the finish line, and in the end, we did not do well. The winds were weak and from the easterly quadrant, with near calms in the middle of the course, and only a taste of the prevailing southwesterlies upon approach to the island. Boat and crew have aged well, but aged nonetheless.

The conditions were not auspicious for a venerable IOR design that at 38 feet LOA, weighs over 10 tons. It was a benign but slow contest, and definitely not a small-boat race. For small, older boats to do well in the Bermuda Race, the ideal scenario is a windy start, pushing the larger racing yachts towards the island, only to be met there by calm conditions, while the smaller, slower boats continue on their course and bring a new, belated breeze with them.

The 2004 edition of the Bermuda Race was a navigator's conundrum. The first part of this Bermuda Race featured light air, followed by a day of northerly winds associated with a frontal passage, followed by a dying easterly, which caught us mid-way, until the wind finally clocked to more reasonable southwesterly breezes as we moved towards the finish line. Accurate weather forecasting played an important role in either success or failure. We had an initial forecast from the Locus weather service, but we did not have reliable electronic access to fast updates. As Nick Nicholson (erstwhile navigator of *Pirate* in the eighties) stated in a recent issue of the magazine *Practical Sailor*, a slow-moving, weak, high-pressure system was the major tactical problem for the race. In his words: "As the high overtook the fleet, the winds would gradually clock through southeast, south, then southwest as the high merged with the usual summer mid-Atlantic high pressure that normally occupies a large portion of the Atlantic basin south and east of Bermuda."

Pirate was sailed well by a crew with high morale, even though we ran out of propane, due to a small leak, in the middle of the course, and had to consume cold meals for three days! After crossing the finish line late in the day, we had to navigate the

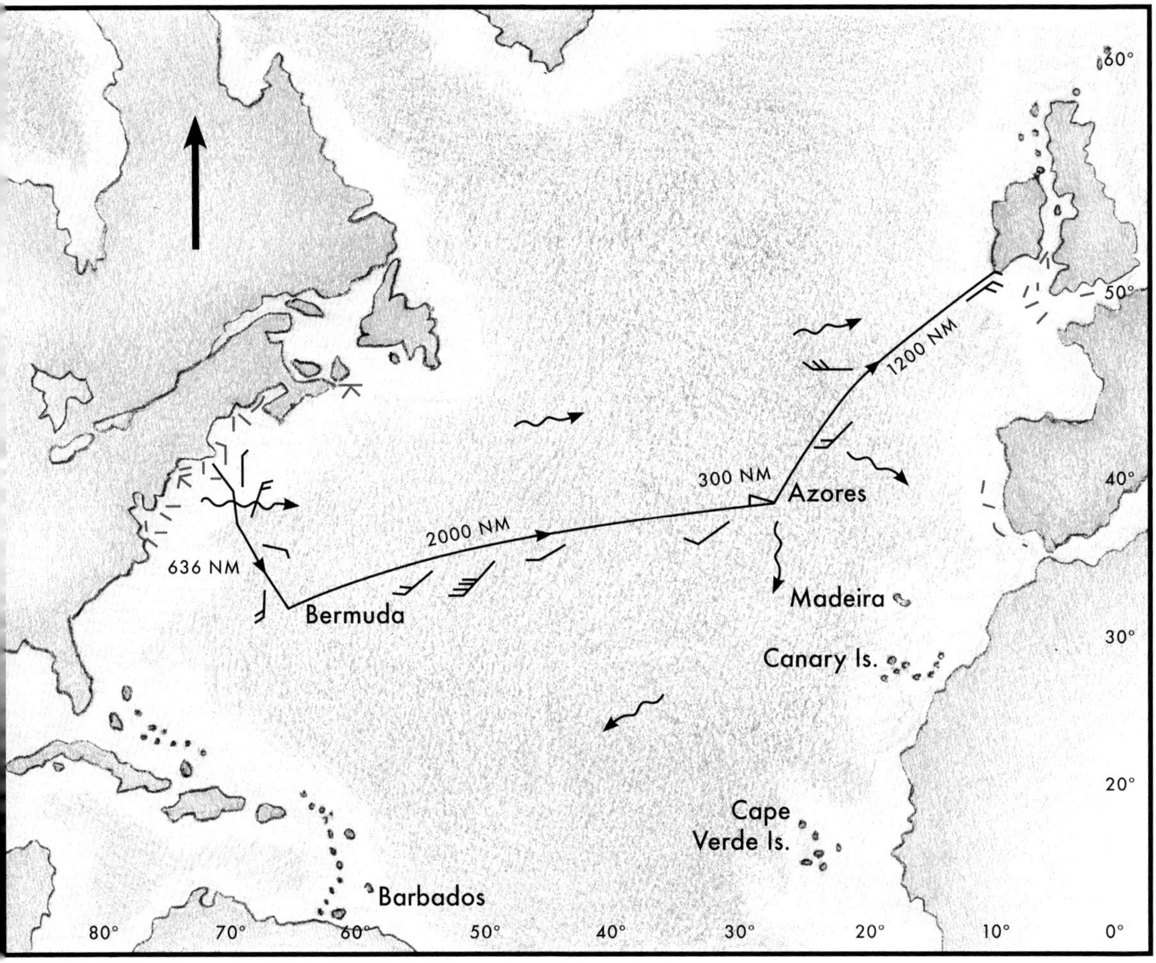

Fourth transatlantic crossing.

narrow channel towards Hamilton in the dark, with contrary winds and choppy seas.

After the 2004 Bermuda Race, and a stay in Bermuda, we planned to take *Pirate* to the Azores. Our performance in the race was not distinguished—a Brit would call it indifferent, or lackluster. Then, in Hamilton, an accident befell the first mate that could have been catastrophic. As we walked one evening along a meandering road, a rushing van hit Christina in the cheek with its side mirror, and downed her in a pool of blood. We rushed her to the hospital where she received her stitches. By the grace of God her eye was spared, and the episode left only a subtle, but permanent, scar.

She bravely insisted that she was ready to cross the Atlantic as soon as her wound was stable. This leg was approximately 2,000 NM long. I was hesitant and concerned, but in the end we set sail toward the Azores. We were only three on board: two men and one woman, Ellery (Tig) Smith, Christina, and myself. Christina's determination and resilience belonged to a tale from an earlier century, the kind spun by Patrick O'Brian. The English are nostalgic about their naval tradition, which mostly comes from an age of sail, 1750-1850, when ships were built from wood, and the sailors who crewed them are portrayed as tough and unyielding, like iron. The phrase "wooden ships and iron men" refers to those times. What about composite yachts and iron women who heal their wounds in the open sea? Our era finally acknowledges, albeit begrudgingly, that bravery is not gendered.

Departing from Hamilton, Bermuda, on July 5, 2004, *Pirate*'s course threaded a fine line beween a high-pressure system with little or no wind to starboard, and a low-pressure system full of sound and fury to port. Twice she was sucked into the vortex of the low. One time night was falling, and we were tired, so we decided to heave to.

Heaving to, an essential sailing skill for every ocean sailor, is a way of slowing a sailboat's forward progress, by parking the boat with the jib aback and the rudder turned to windward so that the boat cannot sail ahead. With this simple technique, you can stop the boat in a controlled manner without having to stay at the helm. It can be a valuable skill for managing a storm because it allows you to "lock" the boat at a safe angle to wind and waves and go below to ride it out. Relax in a storm? It is possible, and the welcome pause allows the crew to regain strength. On *Pirate*, we set the helm and sail so that the boat did not need to be actively steered. As soon as the sails were sheeted at cross purposes, and the wheel secured, the boat relaxed and rode the waves at an angle of 40 degrees to the wind. The maneuver lets the crew go below to enjoy a candlelight supper with wine, as the breezes roar above. In such a position the dangers are two: to be capsized by a rogue wave, or to be hit by another vessel. But the waves were well mannered, and there were few vessels, if any, in the somewhat desolate route from Bermuda to the Azores. Of course, the crew must still be on alert to prevent a rogue wave from capsizing the vessel. The weather improved; *Pirate* was a happy ship again, and resumed her course.

Trace of *Pirate*'s last visit to the Azores (Photo credit: Fernando Oliveira)

With caution, and the sun shining in our eyes on a splendid summer morning, we approached the isle of Faial, of the Azores Central Group, July 22, 2004. In front of the vessel was a large pod of sperm whales. They were a reluctant welcoming committee, peaceful and indifferent. I must concur with what Captain Joshua Slocum wrote in his classic book *Sailing Alone Around the World*: "Only those who have seen the Azores from the deck of a vessel realize the beauty of the mid-ocean picture."

It was *Pirate*'s second visit to Horta in thirteen years, and her stay this time was as pleasant as the first. As in 1991, and as is customary there, I left notice of our passage by putting the name of our boat on a sea wall. But this time I did not paint the letters. (There were no signs of the earlier mural.) Instead they were assembled in a string of mayolica tiles (*azulejos*) and cemented to the wall to leave a more permanent impression. *Azulejo* is an arabic word used in Spain and Portugal to designate a glazed tile: a terracotta tile covered with an opaque glazing. In the Azores *azulejos* have been used since medieval times to decorate walls, fountains, pavements, ceilings, vaults, or fireplaces. I loved my *azulejos* and the way they shone in the sun, showing that *Pirate* was there. The blue tiles were still there in 2018.

A Recollection

Thoughts on many happy voyages on the s/v *Pirate* over the years.

By Robert N. Stewart

There were races and cruises from Long Island Sound, Gulf of Maine, Halifax, Bermuda, The Azores, west coast of Scotland, western Norway to the Arctic Circle, and Antigua and the islands—all done with great shipmates.

The 1997 Halifax Race had the best international cuisine any crew could ever have, where one of the crew (whose name shall be withheld) in an effort to lighten the ship, managed to jettison most all of the silverware and dishes; it still is not known if this helped our position at the finish of the race.

The 2004 Atlantis Cup, the offshore championship series of Portugal, between the islands of the Azores was notable in that a lock was put on the transmission before the start of the first race and was not removed until after the finish of the last race—they must have heard of Ted Hood's comment that only about ten percent of offshore racers don't cheat. These inter-island races saw much macieira consumed (probably the worst brandy in the world), and one of our dauntless crew running with the bulls on Terceira.

These are happy memories of a good boat and even greater friends.

* * *

ROBERT N. STEWART is a veteran of seven Newport–Bermuda Races, eight Marblehead–Halifax Races, and the Atlantis Cup. He worked on New York Harbor tugs for Moran Towing as both a captain and Connecticut River pilot for 20 years and as manager of the Portsmouth division of Moran Towing for 20 years. Stewart is a lifelong sailor and wooden boat owner.

After cruising and racing locally in the Azores, we departed on a second transatlantic leg from the Azores to Ireland, for a length of 1,200 NM.

We departed from San Miguel and then Horta on August 10, 2004, and arrived in Ireland on a dark and stormy evening, August 18. We moved along as the night fell, with the Fastnet Light looming on the horizon, sailing over the wreck of the *Lusitania*, passed the Old Head of Kinsale, and aimed for the yacht club in Crosshaven. We had a welcome reception at the oldest yacht club in the world. In the year 1720, interest in the sport had progressed so much in the British Isles that the 26-year-old William O'Brien, the 9th Lord Inchiquin, and five of his friends got together and established "The Water Club of the Harbour of Cork." Known today as the Royal Cork Yacht Club, it is indeed the oldest yacht club in the world.

The next few days we visited the sights of County Cork; Crosshaven and especially Kinsale can claim their place among Ireland's most historic and attractive locations. In the old days, where we now saw mostly pleasure boats in the harbor, hundreds of fishing boats must have been a common sight. The town itself goes back to the 12th century, when it was founded by the Anglo-Normans. It was a good option to leave *Pirate* at the well-managed and old-fashioned Castlepoint Boatyard, to retrieve her the following summer for more adventures on Irish and Scottish waters.

For *Pirate,* this fourth Atlantic crossing was the end of long ocean voyages and the beginning of coastal adventures, along wild and intriguing shores.

9

The Isles of the North

Wherever we want to go, we go.
That's what a ship is, you know.
It's not just a keel and a hull and a deck and sails;
that's what a ship needs.
But what a ship is... is freedom.

—Captain Jack Sparrow

This chapter contains a series of recollections on a different type of sailing than the voyages described before, with different requirements and in many ways a different mode of being on board. The ocean crossings were voyages of identity, and they marked the soul. The adventures that follow represent an entry into a different world—the cruising world—albeit an exotic one. With *Pirate* it could not be otherwise. Therefore, the narrative tends to veer towards the travelogue, and the land figures more prominently than the immensity of sheer blue water and its moods.

"Two opposing ideas of North repeat (and contradict each other) from European antiquity to the time of the 19th century Arctic explorers: that the North is a place of darkness and dearth, the seat of evil. Or, conversely, that it is a place of austere felicity where virtuous peoples live behind the north wind and are happy." Thus wrote Peter Davidson, in an erudite and poetic book: *The Idea of North*; Peter Davidson; London; Reaktion Books, 2005. For us on board *Pirate* the second idea became reality, as we encountered both austere felicity and virtuous people wherever we sailed. But the imagination sometimes pulled me to the first possibility.

Ireland and Scotland

Taking a sailboat through the Irish Sea, and sailing in the Hebrides, in Scotland, is a challenge and an adventure well worth the effort. Rocks, skerries, tidal falls, fog, and strong winds can test the mettle of ship and crew, but the rewards are sublime seascapes and magic anchorages.

On July 5, 2005, we left Crosshaven on board *Pirate*, and cruised along the eastern coast of Ireland to Dublin, and then to North Ireland, Belfast. We crossed over to Port Ellen, in Islay, Scotland, and then cruised the Inner Hebrides to Oban, to join the 2005 cruise-in-company rally called "The Single Malt Cruise." I have always dreamt of a wee dram in the place where the noble drink is distilled. In 2005 I made it a reality.

The Malts Cruise is a two week summer sailing voyage combining exceptional cruising, beautiful scenery and amazing wildlife with a journey of discovery into the world of Scottish single malt whisky. We nosed it, sampled it, and compared. We shared these delights with good friends, even acquiring a taste for haggis, the national dish. We experienced less delightful Scottish fare: rain, fog, strong currents, and the midges. But when the skies opened and the nosing was good, with smell and taste of peat, Scotland was grand.

A mix of cruising in company and solo exploration was spiced with social events ashore and rendezvous afloat. We explored remote lochs, discovered hidden anchorages, and reveled in the mountain scenery. Whether sharing a dram in the cockpit, enjoying the local seafood or joining a village hall ceilidh (*Ceilidh* (kay-lee) is the Scotch Gaelic word for a "visit," a party or celebration), the Malts Cruise is full of opportunities to meet fellow cruisers and locals. We visited a distillery in the morning, and saw basking sharks in the afternoon. It was a splendid experience, adding structure and good company to West Highland sailing.

We returned to Oban for wintering in August 2005. Our friends, Gary Forster,

Lily Louis, and Bob Stewart, joined us in difficult waters, with strong tides and splendid vistas. Of special notice was rounding the Cape of Ardnamurchan. The Ardnamurchan Peninsula is a wild place with the best scenery on the west coast of Scotland. The area is noted for being unspoiled and undisturbed. There are moorland, forests, lochs and beaches to explore including the magnificent Sanna Bay, and wildlife is all around, from golden eagles to whales and dolphins. We barely saw the ragged coast while facing winds of more than 40 knots. And yet, *Pirate* braved the gusts and we had lots of fun, salty spray, and good whisky, too.

A Recollecion

By Gary Forster

The tale of Pirate *is of world travel but also of the crew who ventured from the sight of land. She carries the experiences, memories and folly of all those who sailed aboard. She was, and still is, a vessel to learn about sailing, the sea, and life.*

I've learned an offshore vessel is a microcosm of life in general, but much more compact. On a well-run boat, the crew must work well together, otherwise discord or worse is possible. Humility is a prized virtue aboard and was reflected in the ship's motto, "So far—So good." A simple verse but open to learning, mistakes and team work. It never failed us.

I have many recollections aboard Pirate, *some on land but mostly at sea. As a result, "situational awareness" has become part of my daily waking hours. Small changes in weather, as well as a pause for a beautiful midnight sunset along the coast of Norway, have made me more attentive to details these days. One particular event while sailing with Juan, Christina, Bob, and my now wife Lily, along the western highland coast of Scotland sits in my memory. In a fresh breeze to windward,* Pirate *was getting rather lively. Juan asked that a reef be put in the main to temper her motion through the waves. One of the crew aboard, a longtime* Pirate *crewmember and friend, Bob Stewart, and I went amidships to tie in a reef. Conditions were becoming more lively, and as we laid in the reef,* Pirate *partially submerged into the next wave. As we stood in water just above our knees we looked at each other and began to laugh. We were just two kids in a very large puddle. Earlier in my sailing career I think I would have been concerned, if not frightened, but* Pirate *and the lessons she taught me had me laughing. The lesson was to always do what's right for the boat and the crew, while having fun.*

I sailed many deliveries, ocean and coastal races aboard Pirate *during the 1990s. After the millennium, sailing to Scotland and on to Norway, I have learned that a boat's personality is forged from those who sail her. Over the years I've noticed you learn more in a passage of a week than you may learn in a decade about a person onshore. Strong bonds are formed that transcend the passage.* Pirate *has taught many people and continues to do so.*

* * *

GARY FORSTER is the Director of Capital Project Management for ABS Partners Real Estate, LLC, in New York City. He is a member of the Cruising Club of America as well as The New York Yacht Club. He served as Chairman of the New York Yacht Club's Seamanship Committee, and has built a number of small to moderate wooden sailing vessels. He and his wife Lily sail a 30-foot catboat out of Oyster Bay and along the New England coast.

In 2005-06 *Pirate* spent the winter laid up in Ardantrive Bay, on the southeast shore of Kerrera, under the cover of a capacious shed that once housed the famed Catalina flying boats, primed to hunt U-boats in World War II.

After so many years and miles, the boat needed a new engine, and we found what we needed in that small island in front of the city of Oban, Kerrera. The able family team of Tony and Lisa Cox, and their capable assistant Tristan Mortimer, at Oban Yachts and Marine Services, removed the decaying Perkins Perama, and installed a new Beta Marine 28 HP.

The island is a beautiful, wild, tenacious piece of real estate with a millennial history, undaunted by modernity. How did an island so small, and so bare, provide sustenance to its inhabitants? Human resourcefulness and ingenuity made the island yield what was needed through the ages. From the island's meadows and hills came an abundance of game (wild ducks and geese, rabbits, and foxes), pasture for cattle,

A wee dram in Talisker, Isle of Skye, Scotland.

barley (called corn) for the mills, crops of flax, and a bounty of milk. Through the centuries there were seven farms in Kerrera. Today, in my long walks on the bogs, I counted only three fully fledged farms.

Before coal was traded, the islanders of Kerrera depended on peat moss to heat their homes, boil the water, and cook meals. Peat was used in the farm kilns to dry the grain, and in the mill to grind it. Peat heated the blacksmith's forge, softened the tar for sheep smearing, and was essential for brewing and distilling, (beer and whisky are close cousins) and for burning lime. There was plenty of stone to build houses, but wood was rare.

Lobsters could be caught near shore. The creatures came into food fashion sometime in the 19th century. In the early 20th, the lobsters of Kerrera—thousands upon thousands of them—supplied the Cunard "Queens," the *Queen Mary* and the *Queen Elizabeth*. The sea also granted valuable plant material on shore. Seaweed was good

In shed at Oban Yachts, in Kerrera.

fertilizer for the land, and kelp, rich in soda, made ash when burned, used in the manufacture of glass, soap and bleaches. The weed was gathered by boat, or on the shore at low tide by wading, cut from rocks and boulders with a toothed sickle, and dragged in with long-handled hooks. Families joined in carrying it up from the shore in creels upon their backs, or with the help of ponies. Then it was laid out to dry upon the grass or on low broad walls loosely built of water-washed stones. Two or three days of sun were enough to make it ready for burning in the kelp kilns. Then the mass of glassy ash was bagged and awaited the arrival of the collecting vessel. (Thousands of sea miles away in the Southern Ocean, the inhabitants of the Falklands or Malvinas, in a similar ecology, did the exact same thing.)

For millennia, this was the routine for many on Kerrera, the history of the common folk. As for the recorded saga, the other history of the powerful few—mostly a story of mayhem and crime—it is said that Alexander II came here in 1249 with a fleet to evict the Norsemen who held Kerrera. He was taken ill and died in Horseshoe Bay.

Kerrera was a droving station between Mull and the mainland. Cattle had to swim across its northern top to the mainland at Oban. Gylen Castle is a ruin on the cliffs overlooking Port a'Chastell on the south coast. Built in 1582, it has an air of Renaissance elegance in its contours.

Going Further North: A Quick Preview over five years

What follows is a quick overview of a spectacular cruise, or set of cruises, in Nordic waters, which took us past 68°North latitude. I use "Nordic" instead of "Scandinavian" because it encompasses countries like Finland and the Netherlands, besides Denmark, Norway, and Sweden, and because these countries try to be as different from one another as possible. To be a Scandinavian is not to be a Scandinavian.

After wintering *Pirate* in the Hebrides, we left Scotland in a grand manner. We departed Oban on July 6, 2006, sailed on the Caledonian Canal and Loch Ness, arriving in Inverness two weeks later, to change crew and continue our cruise to the Orkneys and the Shetland Islands at the end of July.

In August, we left Lerwick, Shetland, and crossed the North Sea, arriving in Bergen, Norway, on August 15. We left the yacht near Bergen for the winter, in the water, where the sea does not freeze, thanks to the Gulf Stream. Bergen is a delightful city; the proud locals say that when God built it, He wanted to keep it clean, so it rains 300 days a year.

In late June 2007, we started a cruise north along the coast of Norway, past the Arctic Circle, visiting the Lofoten islands, and finishing the cruise in the port of Bodø in August, 2007. We left *Pirate* in Bodø for the winter of 2007-08, this time on the hard.

In July 2008, we left Bodø with the mast unstepped, crossed the world's largest whirpool in Saltenfjord, and arrived in the port of Rognan, Norway, where we lifted the yacht and transported her on a truck across Sweden and Lapland to the Yxpila Boatyard in Kokkola, Finland, for wintering and a refit. When the work was done and the sailing season arrived, we readied *Pirate* to explore the delights and the dangers of the northern Baltic Sea.

From May 22 to July 10, 2008, we cruised along the coasts of Finland, the High

Coast of Sweden, the Stockholm archipelago, the Göta Canal, the west coast of Sweden, the lower fjord of Oslo, Norway, and then Denmark, through the Skagerrat and the Kattegat Seas. Then the yacht was transported aboard the MV *Ankergracht* to Palma de Mallorca, where she was sold in July, 2010.

A summary cannot hope to provide flavor—the sights and sounds, the touch and taste that we experienced in those extraordinary years of sailing—nor convey a sense of what we learned.

From Oban to Inverness

As noted before, *Pirate* passed the winter in a shed, on the Isle of Kerrera, near Oban, in the Inner Hebrides, North Scotland. We had the new engine, a superb Beta Marine 28 hp, and a new Autoprop propeller, which proved to be a winning combination of smoothness, speed, and boat control.

In early June, we arrived to test the boat in sea trials. Phil and Beth Steggall, from Jamestown, Rhode Island, arrived, and we set sail to explore the vicinity. We sailed to the Isle of Mull, where we visited the lovely harbor of Tobermory, and then sailed towards the Western entrance to the Caledonian Canal.

Some of the most dramatic scenery on the West Coast, including Britain's highest mountain, are found there. The mountains of the Highlands drop sheer into the sea. Part of the shore combines mountains and sea. Of special interest are Loch Etive and Loch Linnhe. The passage from Oban to Loch Linnhe is sheltered from the west but tides run strongly and careful pilotage is needed at the north end. We spent the first night of this passage at anchor in the peaceful Kentallen Bay (56°38'N, 005°24'W). Then we sailed through the Corran Narrows, past Fort William into the Canal entrance at Corpach, to negotiate the first locks.

About a third of the Caledonian Canal is a man-made cut, linking a series of five natural lochs, including Loch Ness, and crossing the Highlands of Scotland through the Great Glen from Fort William to Inverness. The Canal runs about 50 miles from coast to coast, and passes through magnificent scenery varying from towering mountains with snow-filled gulleys to wooded hillsides and ruined castles steeped in history. There are surprisingly few stopping places for yachts, partly because of the deep water and partly through restrictions by conservationists.

The Caledonian Canal runs in a northeasterly direction from Corpach to Clachnaharry near Inverness, a distance of 60 NM of which 38 are through Lochs Lochy, Oich, and Ness, and the remainder consists of an artificial cut. There are altogether 29 locks rising to a height of 30 meters above sea level at Loch Oich, and ten swing bridges. We did not encounter heavy traffic. In three places the locks are grouped in "staircases" so that yachts arriving have to wait if vessels are already going through the staircases in either direction. Jetties are available at frequent intervals along the canal. We had to wait out a severe gale before sailing through Loch Ness, but after the wind subsided the passage through this famous body of water was uneventful. There were no sightings of the fabled monster Nessie—the legend goes back to the 6th century, but got a boost after the introduction, in the 1930s, of doctored photographs and fake news.

When we reached Inverness, we changed crews, and prepared for a more open sea passage on the North Sea. Our plan was to sail from Inverness to the Orkneys and the Shetlands before crossing over to Norway.

The Pentland Firth is a seaway, which separates Orkney from the Mainland of Scotland. The firth is 11 km wide between Brough Ness on the island of South Ronaldsay and Duncansby Head in Caithness.

Orkney lies between 58°41' and 59°24' North, and 2°22' and 3°26' West, measures 80 km from northeast to southwest and 47 km from east to west, and covers 973 km^2. Excepting on the west coasts of the larger islands, which present rugged cliff scenery remarkable both for beauty and for coloring, the group lies somewhat low and is of bleak aspect.

Orkney consists of about 70 small islands, 16 km north of Caithness in northern Scotland. The largest island in the group is known as the Mainland, with approximately 20 islands being inhabited.

Orkney's administrative capital is Kirkwall, where we docked at a convenient marina. The town has a Hanseatic feeling. The yacht club, with showers and a bar for visiting yachtsmen, is situated in the Girnel, a stone building next to the quay, which dates from 1640 and used to be a corn warehouse in those days. Home to the St Magnus Cathedral, Kirkwall has about 7,500 inhabitants and a large port. The only other burgh is Stromness, with a population of only about 2,000, which is prettier than Kirkwall but less convenient on a passage from the south. The third largest settlement (c. 550) is St Margaret's Hope, on South Ronaldsay.

The hilliest island is Hoy; the highest point in Orkney, Ward Hill, is to be found there. The only other islands containing heights of any importance are the Mainland with (another) Ward Hill, and Wideford Hill and Rousay. Nearly all of the islands possess lochs (lakes), and The Loch of Harray and The Loch of Stenness attain noteworthy proportions. The rivers are merely streams draining the high land. Excepting on the western fronts, the coastline of the islands is deeply indented, and the islands themselves are divided from each other by straits generally called "sounds" or "firths."

The very names of the islands indicate their nature: the terminal "a" or "ay" represents the Norse ey, meaning "island," which is scarcely disguised in their names today. Unknown to us at the time, to the west and not along our course lay the isle of Vesterey in Norse, or Westray in current English. It is known for being the most go-ahead of the islands, actively adapting its society and economy to the changing times, from fishing and farming to tourism. In 1969 a yawl named *Westray* visited her namesake island with one of the island's descendants at the helm. Glenn MacNary had commissioned the yawl from the Concordia Company in 1960, and was on his way to Norway. As fate would have it, I am the present owner of that yawl.

The islets are usually styled "holms" and the isolated rocks "skerries." The tidal currents, or "roost" (as some of them are called locally, from the Icelandic) off many of the isles run with enormous velocity—up to 12 knots on spring tides, and whirlpools are a frequent occurrence, and strong enough to prove a source of danger to small craft.

The charm of Orkneys does not lie in their ordinary physical features, so much as in beautiful atmospheric effects, extraordinary examples of light and shade, and rich coloration of cliff and sea.

The islands are notable for the lack of trees, which is partly accounted for by the amount of wind (although the climate is temperate). The formation of peat is evidence that this was not always the case, and deliberate deforestation is believed to have taken place at some stage prior to the Neolithic; the use of stone in settlements such as Skara Brae is evidence of the lack of timber for building.

Most of the land is still taken up by farms, and agriculture is the most important sector of the economy, with fishing also a major occupation. Orkney exports beef, cheese, whisky, beer, and seafood.

A BIT OF HISTORY

It is easy to forget that for much of history the sea has been less a barrier to movement than a highway that promoted it. To Scottish eyes, Kirkwall may seem a distant northerly outpost. To the Norse at the end of the first millennium, it lay at the heart of a culture linking Scandinavia with Iceland, Shetland, the Western Isles, Argyll, parts of Ireland and the Isle of Man. For this seafaring empire, Kirkwall was at the very center of their world.

Less than two miles south of Kirkwall lies the famous British Navy anchorage of Scapa Flow. Scapa Flow is a natural harbor, used over many centuries, from the Viking fleet of King Haokon in the 13th Century, to the present day. It formed an important northern base for the British fleets in both world wars.

During the First World War, the British Grand Fleet used Scapa Flow as a northern base. After a German U-Boat managed to enter the Flow early in the war, merchant ships were sent as block ships in strategic places and anti-submarine nets were put in place. From this base, vessels from the fleet made sweeps in search of the enemy.

After the armistice, 74 ships of the German High Seas Fleet were ordered into Scapa Flow to be interned. They arrived in November 1918, and stayed there for 10 months. During this time, they became a tourist attraction, with boat trips to see them. By June 1919, Rear Admiral von Reuter, the German officer in command at Scapa Flow, knew that Germany would have to accept surrender terms. When the main part of the British Fleet left Scapa for exercises he gave the order for the German fleet to be scuttled. They blew up and sank the ships. Today visitors can buy a black T-shirt that mocks the episode, and reads: "German Admiral to his captains: Idiots! I said *gentle retreat*, not *scuttle the fleet*."

During World War II, the Home Fleet was based at Scapa Flow, from where it helped to protect the Arctic Convoys to Murmansk.

In October 1939, only a month after war had been declared, an assault on Scapa Flow was planned using the U-Boat U-47, commanded by Lieutenant Günter Prien. On the night of October 13th, the U-Boat managed to pass between the Orkney Mainland and Lamb Holm into Scapa Flow, between two northerly block ships. Just after midnight the U-Boat sighted *HMS Royal Oak* in Scapa Bay. Torpedoes were fired, making a hole 30 feet in diameter in the hull, and she capsized. From a crew of 1400, 833 men lost their lives. *HMS Royal Oak* is a protected war grave, and memorial services are conducted each year on the anniversary of the sinking.

Fair Isle

From Kirkwall we sailed to Fair Isle, wild and interesting, with only a small tenable harbor. Long ago, the cultivable land and the better grazing were divided into small crofts. To this day crofting is a system that gives each household a stake in the island and its future. It is a lifestyle based on low-intensity, subsistence farming. The combination of modern technology and old-style labor produces hay, silage, oats, kale, and turnips as winter fodder for sheep and cattle.

Although Fair Isle is so far north, islanders can grow a lot of their own food outside—potatoes and a wide range of vegetables. Increasingly, crops for household use are raised under glass and polytunnels.

This account would not be complete without mentioning the encounter with some vicious pirate birds of the North Sea. Walking to the north-end lighthouse, we were subject to aerial attack from aggressive Arctic Skuas guarding their nests. In Britain the Arctic Skua is confined to breeding in north and west Scotland, which is the southern extremity of its circumpolar, high latitude breeding range. They are large, powerful birds, and they make a direct attack to defend their breeding grounds. They dive on people walking to the bird sanctuary like Stuka bombers. Both skuas and harriers share the same breeding grounds, but harrier nests are exposed to the sky and vulnerable to raids from the more aggressive birds. As a result, the numbers of harriers have declined and those of skuas have increased. We walked those moors with a stick, so that the birds would hit the stick before they could take a piece of our scalps. At one point, I defended myself using the stick as a baseball bat—my sole but effective defense.

Shetland

After our visit we set sail for the Shetland Islands, some 45 NM from Fair Isle. Bressay Sound, the sheltered stretch of water between the Mainland of Shetland and the island of Bressay, now looks an obvious place for a harbor. But until around 1625 there were just a few huts here gathered around a leir-vik, Norse for "muddy bay." The wealth brought by the herring fishery allowed a major planned expansion of Lerwick, focused on the fine Town Hall.

Today Lerwick is a fascinating blend of the old and the new. It is a large and busy working port, and the terminus for the NorthLink ferries to Kirkwall and Aberdeen. Ferries to other destinations in Scandinavia, Faroe, and Iceland are also regular visitors, and the Bressay Ferry operates from here. At the north end of the port is the Böd of Gremista, a fishing shack from the 1700s now open in summer as a museum.

The North Sea.

The North Sea (historically known as the German Ocean) is a sea of the Atlantic Ocean, located between Norway and Denmark in the east, the United Kingdom in the west, and Germany, the Netherlands, Belgium, and France in the south. An offshoot of the North Sea is the Skagerrak, between Denmark, Norway, and Sweden, which connects to the Baltic Sea through the Kattegat, Öresund, the Great Belt, and the Little Belt. In the south, the North Sea connects with the rest of the Atlantic through the Strait of Dover into the English Channel and in the north through the Norwegian Sea.

The name conjured up swelling mounds of black water crested by foam and pockmarked by rain. This sea is frequently stormy, heavily tidal, and shallow. Yet, as we got a good weather window, we found this pesky old sod of a sea calm, if foggy, and the color of the water was an attractive mixture of grey, green, and blue. We were lucky. Only north of the Shetlands does the depth reach 100 fathoms. A shallow sea in a storm means square waves, or breaking waves—no fun at all. We were spared that mess.

To take advantage of a favorable weather window, we cast off on July 5th, across the North Sea on a course due east from Lerwick to reach central Norway, near the city of Bergen and the beautiful fjords leading to it.

Leaving Lerwick in thick fog, with the ebbing tide, we got a push of one knot. The wind clocked from southeast to southwest, and was gentle, Force 3 to 4. We sailed and motorsailed at 6.5 knots over the ground. When the fog lifted, we saw a fair amount of traffic—we had some close calls with tankers, tenders to the oil rigs, and large fishing ships.

After sailing overnight (an overstatement, since the gloaming continues in the summer from one day to the next) we sighted Norway, entered the fjord that leads to the city of Bergen, and docked at a marina in the village of Hjellestad. The passage took 44 hours.

For millennia, the North Sea has been a vital trading pool for Northern Europe, as well as a fertile fishing ground. More recently, it has provided reserves of natural gas and oil that have benefited Britain and Norway in a big way. The North Sea reeks of history, legends, and sagas of good and ill repute. In the 8th and 9th centuries, it provided passage for the raiders who plundered the British Isles, and reached the Mediterranean on one end of the world, and Newfoundland (perhaps even Rhode Island and Massachusetts) on the other. The most famous were the Vikings, who paddled enthusiastically across the North Sea in their long ships and set about stealing, looting, raping, pillaging, and burning until William the Conqueror put an end to all that. They were violent pirates, but also great shipwrights and splendid navigators.

Today the heirs of the Vikings are a very civilized bunch, local, communal, cosmopolitan and friendly, all in one. Norway, their country, is spectacular. It boasts one of the most beautiful and lengthy coastlines in the world. If one could stretch it in a single line, it would circle the earth one and a half times! Norway is a large country where there are fewer people (4.48 million) than in either London or New York. Today they live healthily and well.

Fjords and Islands

When foreigners speak about Norway it is generally about fjords, and the fjords are impressive, but somewhat monotonous. When you have been in one you have been in them all. Few people are sailing in the fjords in Norway; many Norwegians think

This is how Norwegians built ships 1200 years ago, and still do!

the islands are more beautiful. Those who have had boats for years and think about holidays never think of taking them in a fjord. One of the reasons is that, as in a lake, winds in the fjords are either scant or violent, and unpredictable. Moreover, there is no place to anchor. A fjord is deep; there is no island, no beach, only the rugged mountains that drop thousands of feet into the water. By contrast, the most popular place for sailors is the area from Maloy to Stavanger, with thousands of islands and beaches. It is spectacular, quiet, and nice. Another equally legendary area is the Lofoten islands, in the Arctic Circle, known for its fishing grounds—not only to humans but to hundreds of killer whales as well. Those were the destinations of *Pirate* in the summer of 2007.

On the other hand, the inhabitants of the villages along the fjords have something in common with sailors. The ground is so steep there are no roads in. The only communication is by sea. (This was also the case with the outports of Newfoundland, before their decimation by ill-conceived industrialization schemes.) As a result most Norwegians are marine-orientated: so much depends on water, and on the habit of self-reliance in small groups, cut off from the rest of humanity, the basic experience of sailors offshore.

Norway seems to be a family- and community-centered society, where the many children one sees rely on themselves at a very early age—they handle boats alone with skill and no fear at all. Someone with greater knowledge of the country may correct me, but these were my first impressions after living aboard in a village marina for a week or so, and talking to young and old either in my broken Norwegian or in their quite good English.

Pirate rested placidly in a nice marina, and in the care of an able seaman, Ørjan Wollertsen, until we resumed our adventures the following summer, toward the Arctic Circle and the magnificent Lofoten Islands.

The Dark Side

What of the dark side of the North? It is the inevitable counterpart of the first, auspicious side of the idea of the North as hope and adventure. It is a sense of hardship and death. During war, this sense of doom is spiced by the addition of perfidy and betrayal. In June 1916, Lord Kitchener, the British Minister of War, arrived in Scapa Flow to visit Admiral Jellicoe and hear his account of the Battle of Jutland. Kitchener then left on board the *Hampshire*, and sailed up the west coast of Orkney. Near Birsay, the *Hampshire* struck a mine, and only 12 men out of 737 survived. On 1926, money was raised by public subscription to erect the Kitchener Memorial at Marwick Head near Birsay.

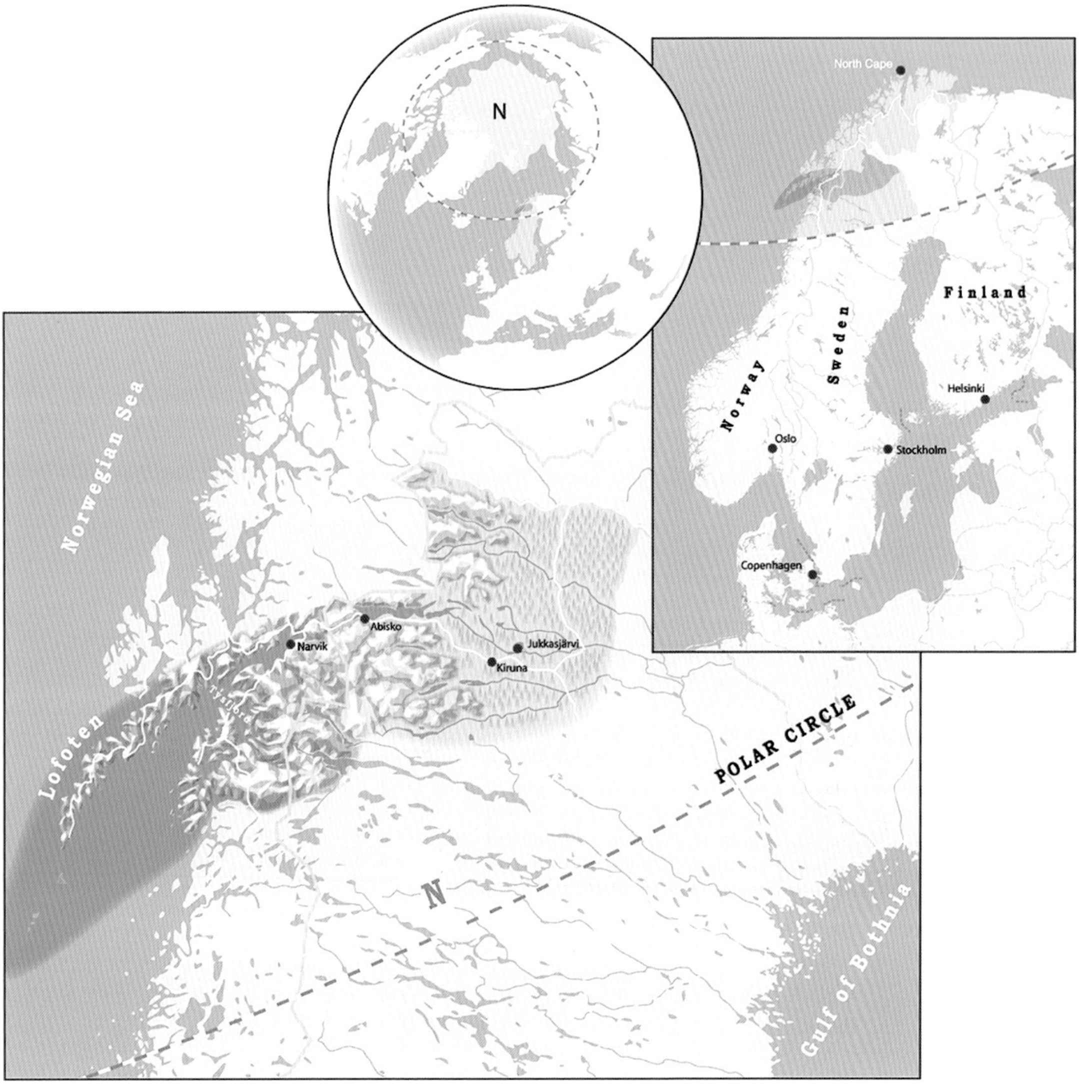

Pirate's sailing grounds for five years.

10

Viking Waters and the Artic Circle

Pretty didn't do it justice. I felt like we'd sailed into a world meant for much larger beings, a place where gods and monsters roamed freely.

—Rick Riordan

A Sea of Surprises

Our boat was old, but fine and strong. The previous winter of 2007 she stayed in the water near the Norwegian city of Bergen. We left Bergen in mid-June, and finished our cruise in the city of Bodø, two months later. We covered just under 900 NM of coastal waters in a northeasterly direction, passed the Arctic Circle, and entered a realm of legend and the sublime.

The further north we sailed, the more spectacular it got. The mountains drop abruptly into the water; they are the most numerous of any country in Europe, and they festoon a sea as deeply blue as the Aegean. The northern coasts still bear the impression of the enormous glaciers that covered them during the Ice Ages and created a split, craggy landscape. Fjords developed by the action of glaciers, which dragged their way through them from the highlands, scraping deep trenches in the land. During the subsequent rise in sea level, they filled with water. They are much deeper than the North Sea.

Above the Arctic Circle, there is at least one day in the summer when the sun never sets, which means that there are more hours of sunlight than in any other cruising destination. Dawn follows immediately on the dusk. The suspension of time, the long night that is never dark, makes for new and sometimes strange behavior. No one sleeps, hardly anyone goes to bed. The young people escape in dinghies and fast boats, and drink a lot. The endless light after dinner gives time for endless parties and, as in a Bergman film, or Shakespearean frolics against a background of impending doom, the long winter that will inevitably arrive. As Peter Davidson writes, "Much of the melancholy of the north arises from the impossibility of saving one minute from the long light against the approaching darkness." (Davidson, *The Idea of the North*, p.131.)

Cruising Norwegian waters is surprising. The Gulf Stream bathes these shores, prevents ice from forming in winter, and stuns the visitor with white sandy beaches and transparent water on some islands, and skerries at high latitudes!

Along the Norwegian coast flows the Norwegian Current. It moves at a depth of 165 to 330 feet. The fresh water contributed by the rivers and the fjords results in a relatively low salinity. A part of the warmer water flowing in from the Atlantic turns northwards again along the coast and results in a warmer stream through the colder waters. In winter the Norwegian Current has a temperature of 36° to 41°F and the salinity is below 34.8 ppt. The Atlantic water in the North Sea, divided from the Norwegian Current by a front, is generally over 43°F with a salinity of 35 ppt. That summer we registered sea temperatures between 50 and 55°F.

The Norwegian Sea is a body of water you learn to fear and respect. Not too long ago (before they became rich with oil), most Norwegians eked out a meager living from fishing. On average, one of every four of those rugged fishermen never returned from the sea. The contours of the sea bottom near the coast, and the clash of contrary currents, makes some areas truly dangerous, so much so that gale warnings are issued by the Norwegian weather service at Beaufort Force 7, instead of Force 8, as is usual in other parts of the world, because of large and irregular waves in such spots. The wave energy in those areas is such that the probability of encountering large seas is much greater than in other areas. Over the course of 12 years, 466 such extreme waves were measured by radar in the North Sea.

Midnight sun in the Lofoten Islands.

At the end of the 1970s a research project localized 24 dangerous areas along the Norwegian coast. They are marked in the pilotage series titled *Den norske los*, which we found an indispensable guide to navigation, despite the language barrier. Earlier volumes of this publication had Norwegian and English text; new editions are in Norwegian only. This is the detailed standard work for both commercial and leisure boating, illustrated with charts and excellent photographs. With milder wind patterns in the summer, it is possible to plan the crossing of those dangerous areas in calm weather. We were among the beneficiaries of this research, which taught us prudence.

Going north, we had to sail the stretch of coast between the two most feared spots: the headland of Stattlandet and the area known as Hustadvika, where the off-shore route is as hazardous as the inner passage between islets and skerries. We waited for good weather and clear visibility, used the most detailed charts we could find, and went offshore. The sea gods were kind and our passage uneventful. Yet this sort of cruising gives a poignant meaning to the expression "between a rock and a hard place."

It is far more difficult to predict and avoid extreme waves occurring in the open ocean. On January 1, 1995 an extreme wave was measured under an oil platform. The maximal amplitude was 57 feet and the maximal wave height 78 feet!

Storms pound northwestern Norway in the winter months. It is not unusual for winds to hit more than 50 knots, gusting to 70. Luckily these events are much less frequent in the summer, when light winds from the northeast or northwest are prevalent. Moreover, the coast affords the seaman the possibility of making progress in the inner passages between the islands and the continent. The light air, the wind direction (frequently on the nose), and the narrow passages make navigation a real challenge, and motoring a frequent necessity.

Given such conditions, it is not surprising to learn that the locals mostly favor 30-foot double-ended powerboats, made of wood or fiberglass. Many of the fishing boats, even up to 80 feet, have varnished wooden hulls with painted wood or aluminum deckhouses.

What did surprise us is how few pleasure boats are seen in these spectacular cruising waters. We saw very few yachts, usually from Scandinavian countries, the Netherlands, Germany, and the UK, and spotted only one American boat in Alesund. The experience takes an American cruiser back 50 years, when harbors were not congested, and the Corinthian, that is purely amateur, spirit was the rule.

As for life on shore in these extreme latitudes, lakes and fjords are punctuated by summer cottages (we were guests in two of them in Norway and in Finland). Every year Scandinavians move northward to these small summer abodes, which they proudly keep as simple as possible, in contrast to the American desire of city comforts in the wild. A central feature of Nordic identity is the summer retreat to a cabin with an outhouse and no running water.

Lessons Learned

Navigation in Norway's inside waters requires constant vigilance. There is a lot of commercial traffic at all hours, thousands of navigational markers of all types—some dating back to the Vikings. Many of the channels are narrowed by rocks and reefs. Americans must always remind themselves that here it is "Red LEFT Returning." Passing one mark on the wrong side means running into rock! On one occasion, rounding the dangerous Statt headland, I thought I sighted whales, but my crew, composed of Lauretta Bruno and Christina Spellman, insisted that they were unmarked rocks. I realized my mistake, and to save face, I declared them "stationary whales" and gave them a wide berth!

Navigation gave us a real workout. We laid out the courses, distances and waypoints the evening before the next day's leg. Sometimes this took up to three hours, with as many as 20 waypoints and 5 charts! After punching the waypoints into the two GPS systems on board, I read them out to at least one other crew member to verify the data. I also entered them on a portable chartplotter to verify our position from time to time, especially when coming to a port or anchorage, using Navionics charts. It helped avoid errors as we could see the route being mapped out on the electronic charts and could quickly determine any inaccuracies. The portable chartplotter can be taken into the cockpit so the helmsman can follow the yacht's progress. In addition to all these procedures, I wrote down all waypoints, courses and distances in a notebook, which I labeled "Book of Courses."

Contrary to the opinion of some friends, I find the Norwegian charts very useful. To take advantage of them, you must learn some rudimentary Norwegian, as well the unique notation and navigational aids systems. The back of every full-size Norwegian chart has a complete catalogue of charts, including a geographical plan of coverage and official hydrographic publications. There is a main chart series, a coastal chart series, and a harbor chart series. However, even the most detailed ones fail to mark every little rock. The Norwegian Hydrographic Society warns that uncharted rocks can be found in areas that have not been surveyed. So, beware—and use a magnifying glass!

On board, we carried no less than 100 navigational charts, and we found them indispensable. Norwegian charts can be purchased in bookstores all along the coast. At

30 US dollars a chart, this represents a small fortune. We were lucky to avail ourselves of the kind offer from a friend in Bergen, who lent us most of the charts we needed. One more warning: the Norwegian charts are only gradually being brought up to the world standard norm, WGS84. There are still many charts both at the old Norwegian datum or the European datum. The datum difference can mean a discrepancy of 100 to 500 meters. To make things even more challenging, we noticed that while sailing in the fjords or near mountains, the compass deviation changed wildly, due to metal masses nearby. A fluxgate compass and a frequent comparison with GPS data are essential. This was truly the area of "magnetic cruising."

I learned navigation in the days of the sextant and RDF. I learned it from a great friend, sailing companion, and old curmudgeon, who mistrusted any novel gizmo that distracted him from paper charts, compass bearings, dead reckoning, and the divine art of celestial Lines Of Positions. That summer I used all the wonderful new tools but realized that they too, like the more primitive (and more reliable) tools of yesteryear, are just that: only tools.

The organic root of navigation is the same today as it was in the old days, and it is only surpassed by the more advanced systems used by whales and sea birds, not by electronics. It consists in being able to look at something from a distance and say what it is. The point is to never stop using your eyes, your calculating brain, and your "sea sense." On the screen everything becomes a game. But hitting a rock is not a game. You have to figure out what you are looking at and relate it to the chart on an ongoing basis, just as my old curmudgeon friend taught me.

This can be an intense process, particularly when you are sailing where you have never been before, in a language you have never spoken, with weather patterns, barometric idiosyncrasies, and compass deviations that you have never encountered before. In short: always rely on your eyes first and then use every means available to confirm what you see. The traditional skills should never be the "backup" method; they are the first method. Everything else is the backup.

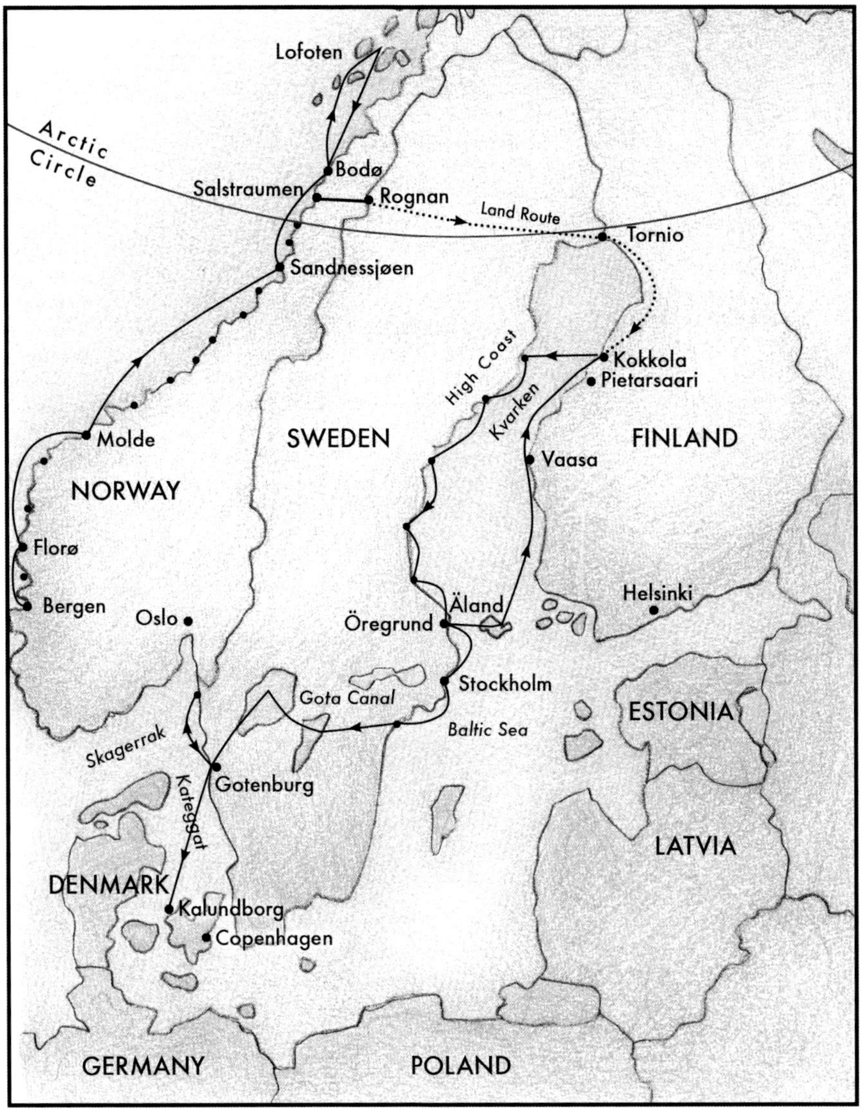

Scandanàvian cruising.

Crossing the Circle: Bob Stewart celebrates.

The Joys of Nordic Sailing

Despite all the difficulties, cruising in Norway is well worth the effort. It has an added advantage: necessity turns you into an honorary Norwegian—serious, fiercely independent, alert, active, and a good seaman. In the background, not Big Brother, but Good Brother is watching: the Norwegian Lifeboat Service (NRSS) is a voluntary organization with some state funding that operates fast rescue boats. Full-time three-person professional crews operate on a rotation system, living on board, and ready to save boats and lives at a moment's notice. I was so impressed that I joined. The cost of annual membership is reasonable. It gives entitlement to services including escort around dangerous headlands, a tow to the nearest harbor, and the first hour of a diver's time without charge. As a member, I received a useful book, which is a compilation of harbor plans. The NRSS is a model organization in a model society.

In 2006, the year of our cruise, the weather improved as we sailed north. Whereas

Ultima Thule: the magical isles.

South Norway had a wet and cold season, in the North we encountered days when the temperature rose to near 30°C (86°F) on sandy beaches—except the water was too cold for swimming.

Ours was an arduous cruise, rewarded at the end by a splendid tour of the Lofoten islands. The excellent weather and the close proximity of the islands to each other made sailing a pleasure. The seas in the Arctic Circle are the finest blue I have ever encountered as a sailor, with the possible exception of the Aegean.

At long last, on August 10th, we docked at the marina in a northern city that is a service and transportation hub, and an important military base. A few days later we hauled out at the local boatyard. *Pirate* was tucked away for the off-season. We left her protected from the fierce southwest winds of the winter, waiting for her mast to be unstepped and a tent to shield the deck from the snow. The following year we planned to sail her to Sweden and the Baltic Sea.

RECOLLECTION

Pirate's Full Norwegian Itinerary

From the ship's log
June 16–August 15, 2007

Ports of call

Norway's coastal ferry service is operated by two companies: Hurtigruten, with 7 ships, and Havila, with 4. On *Pirate* we pretty much followed their scheduled itinerary.

1. Bergen/Askoy 16/06 60°24'N, 5°19'E

Bergen is a beautiful city with a distinct climate that visitors find annoying and the locals say is a blessing: it rains most days of the year. Here Norwegian is spoken with a gutural French-like "r." Its citizens claim that when He created Bergen, God was so impressed that He wanted it washed clean every day.

2. Askoy Sailforening 26/06 60°27'N, 5°03.6'E

Pirate was hauled out at the local sailing club to clean her bottom and get a fresh coat of antifouling paint. She stood in front of a replica Viking ship that had just come from a cruise to Iceland, with a bunch of happy youths dressed in furs as in the old days.

3. Fedje 60°47'N, 4°42.4'E

Fedje is a wonderful westerly island community, with a charming village.

4. Floro 29/06 114 88NM 61°36'N, 5°02'E

With little or no wind, we motorsailed to this port between two fjords. Floro is one of the ferry ports along the "Express Route" and though small, it is fairly cosmopolitan.

5. Kalvåg 31/06 61°45.9'N, 4°52.7'E

We stopped in this fishing village to have a fuel line repaired by a local mechanic. We were told that Kalvåg is the best-kept village in western Norway, and indeed the village has a unique collection of old waterfront buildings, nicely restored. Around the bay, the sea houses are clustered together, and provide a cozy and welcoming atmosphere for sailors.

6. Måløy 03/07 to **Stadlandet** 61°56'N, 5°07'E

Måløy is one of the most important fishing ports in Norway. The town square has a monument remembering the citizens of local municipalities who died in World War II, when Norway offered stiff resistance to the Germans. More densely populated than other ports we visited, it is neat and has spectacular views of the sea and fjords. For us it was the stepping stone to brave the feared Stadlandet. Stadlandet is a peninsula in the northwestern part of Sogn og Fjordane county. The peninsula is considered the dividing point between the Norwegian Sea to the north and the North Sea to the south, and is reputed to be surrounded by fierce and treacherous waters, especially in winter. We were lucky to round this cape on a very calm day. I mistook some rocks for whales, and was corrected by the crew. To save face I called them "stationary whales."

7. Fosnavag 04/07 62°20.5'N, 5°38.4'E

This port is active not only in fishing but in ship building as well, and is connected to other localities by a web of bridges.

8. Ålesund 05/07 62°28.3'N, 6°09.2'E

Ålesund's Art Nouveau architecture is stunning. The turrets, spires and beautiful ornamentation are like something from a fairytale. It is an important city, and an architectural jewel untouched by the ravages of war. Christina, Lauretta Bruno and I left *Pirate* at her dock and took the coastal boat to Geiranger Fjord, for some of the most majestic views of the entire Norway, and just in time to savor the strawberries offered to visitors by local children.

9. Molde 06/07 62°44'N, 7°10'E

Back from Geiranger, in Molde we bid farewell to our friend Lauretta and waited for weather to improve. During our visit, Robert, the local bus driver, saw *Pirate* at the dock and remembered when we met in 2005 during the Single Malt Cruise in Scotland. I don't know how he managed to park the bus and come running down to the seaside to say hello!

10. Kristiansund 11/07 63°07'N,7°44'E

Christina and I sailed through the Hustadvika passage, considered one of the most dangerous parts of the Norwegian coast. We had no trouble and arrived in Kristiansund to meet our friends Gary Forster and Lily Lewis. It was a joy to have them on board again. After a simple oil change and a pleasant meal, the four of us were ready to sail further North.

11. Brekstad 12/07 63°41'N, 9°40'E

This seemed to us a rather somber port, and worth a stop to consider sailing to Trondheim, the old capital of Norway, which in the end we did not do.

12. Kuringsvagen 13/07 64°02.4'N, 10°03'E

The town is, by contrast to Brekstad, a welcoming place with a cozy marina, and a good starting point for boats going to the Lofoten islands. We encountered contrary winds after leaving and decided to return to harbor and wait for better sailing conditions.

13. Rorvik 16/07 64°51'N, 11°13'E

Our old friend and sailing mate, Bob Stewart, joined us in this port. He arrived early and waited for us in the comfort of a Norwegian sea rescue boat, the crew of which he had befriended. They offered him a shower and a berth!

14. Leka 17/07 65°05.2'N, 11°44'E

Another lonely place along the coast, but a good harbor of refuge in stormy weather.

15. Bronnoysund 20/07 65°28'N, 12°12'E

Lily and Gary left us in this coastal city and went to visit relatives who lived nearby. Christina, Bob Stewart, and I took off for the far North, and were lucky to have favorable winds and blue skies.

16. Sandnessjøen 21/07 66°01'N, 12°38'E

This town is located on the island of Alsta, just west of the The Seven Sisters mountain range. For us it was the last port of call before crossing the Arctic Circle.

17. Bolga 22/07 67°17'N, 14°22'E

What a joy to cross the Circle with fair winds and in great spirits, as we sailed past Bolga to points further North!

18. 23/07 66°48'N, 13 14°'E

We made new friends and cruised this area of magical islands in the direction of the Lofoten archipelago.

19. Reine 30/07 67°56.2'N, 13°05'E

No words can do justice to the spectacle of the Lofoten Isles, especially in good weather, and we were graced with splendid weather. Reine is perhaps the most spectacular of these isles: a mountain and a village emerging from a pale blue sea.

20. Aa 67°52.9'N, 12°59.5'E

A charming fishing village, with a very special museum: the museum of cod fish, and the story of a discovery of a dried form of sustenance and a trade that changed the world.

21. Nusfjord 01/08 68°01'N, 13°21'E

On the ship's log I simply wrote: "A fantastic area." In these waters you can imagine giants, and monsters, and mermaids.

22. Stamsund 02/08 68°07.7'N, 13°51'E

23. Henningsvaer 68°09.2'N, 14°12'E

These are all ports that are abuzz in the winter with the cod fisheries, in the cold and in the dark. It has been going on for centuries and has been the subject of many yarns for Davy Jones.

24. Kabelvaag 03/08 68°12.6'N, 14°29'E

This port sports a bar that boasts of serving 100 varieties of whisky, accompanied by a fare of whale meat. Here we made new friends among Norwegian cruisers.

In our Lofoten expedition we had on board two Italian brothers who are more than friends, they are also like brothers to us. Bruno and Paolo Bruni flew from Naples and Tuscany to be with us on *Pirate* in what turned out to be an unforgettable cruise. We fished, we walked the sandy beaches of the North, and we treated ourselves to the luxuries of a spa, with dinner and sauna, in the town of Nyvagar.

25. Trollfjord 68°21'N, 14°56'E

We sailed and motored into this narrow fjord, amazed by the seascape and the mountains.

26. Skrova 04/08 68°10'N, 14°40'E

On the dinghy we did some fishing and sampled the beaches. Nothing compares to gunkholing in the Arctic regions.

27. Helnessund 06/08 67°43.7'N, 14°45'E

More beauty to behold and fishes to catch.

28. Kjerringoy 07/08 67 31'N, 14°45'E

Why did I write "pure beauty" in the log book? Because the place takes one back to the 19th century. It is the best preserved trading post and a journey back in time, with "jektefart" and fish trading, herring and the life as it was in bygone times. This is Norway as it was far away and long ago.

29. Bodø 08/08 67°17'N, 14°22'E

It was the end of a memorable cruise. The crew left and *Pirate* was hauled for the winter.

3/08

An oil change and haul out. We left *Pirate* on the hard at Jakhelln Boatyard, in the town of Bodø, which is pleasant and, among other things, a NATO base.

Total engine hours: 156

TOTAL NAUTICAL MILES 846 cruising miles + 30 odd ones = 876

11

The Shortest Route: to Finland by Fjord and Land

Alku aina hankala, lopussa kiitos seisoo.
The beginning is always difficult, in the end stands the thank.

—Finnish proverb

Back in New York I wrote a letter to our Finnish friend, Lars Colliander, who had provided us with a lot of useful and enthusiastic information about his native land, unyielding Suomi, its history and its waters.

25 July 2008

Dear Lars,

Having returned from Europe, I wish to tell you that my wife Christina and I had a great and successful adventure on sea and land, taking our yacht Pirate *from Bodø and Rognan, Norway to Kokkola, Finland, where she is now at the Yxpila Boat Yard ready for a thorough refit during this fall and winter, and supervised by the original Nautor yard in nearby Jakobstadt.*

Our plans include launching her in "as new" condition next June 2009, and a sail down the Baltic, first through the high coast of Sweden, and then to the Aland archipelago, which you so well described last spring at your house. We liked Finland so much that we plan to spend (hopefully) more than one summer cruising its waters.

We returned to New York from Helsinki, not before touring the waters near the city on a tourist boat, and taking a peek at the lovely Nylandska Jaktklubben, where we hope to dock sometime next summer.

I wish to thank you again for all the information you provided, and will, if you do not mind, call upon your advice again during the year, before returning to the Gulf of Bothnia.

Here are images of our adventure:

Entering the Salstraumen. Mast unstepped and resting on styrofoam blocks.

Pirate goes home by truck from Norway.

Pirate arrives in Kokkola, Finland.

Strange as it may sound, for us it was the shortest route to a desired goal: to have the boat refitted by the hands that had built her, in the Gulf of Bothnia, the Yxpila Boat Yard. I did not supply Lars with details, some of which were extraordinary, and worth telling.

To reach our goal, we had to motor, mast unstepped, through one of the toughest tidal streams in the world, Saltstraumen Maelstrom, to a remote ghost town, Rognan, at the end of a 90-mile-long and solitary fjord. My expressions are not hyperbolic, and the illustrations below may give a glimpse of the extraordinary adventures of *Pirate* in the North. The strangest adventure was traversing the great maelstrom between tides, the only moment when its turbulent waters are calm. The Saltstraumen ranks with the most powerful of all maelstroms.

Malström, or malström/malstrøm in the Scandinavian language, is the combination of *mala*, meaning to grind, and *ström*, meaning current: a crushing current indeed! Located in Nordland, 16 NM east of the city of Bodø, a narrow channel connects the outer Saltfjord with the large Skjerstadfjord, which has the strongest tidal current in the world. Up to 400 million m^3 tons of seawater force their way through a 1.6 NM long and ¼ mile wide strait, every six hours, with water reaching speeds of 20 knots. Vortices up to 30 feet in diameter and 15 feet deep at the eye of the vortex are formed when the current is at its strongest. With the help of Bjorn, a sailor friend born and raised in the area, we managed to time it right: we motored through the vortex as if it were the most placid of lakes. In the opposite direction was a coastal cargo ship with a suggestive name: the *Cabal*. The Norwegian government has a woman on retainer to help pilot ships through the whirlpool—a modern Madame Defarge of coastal navigation.

After that narrow passage, we cruised in an empty fjord for almost 90 miles until we reached the end, where the following day *Pirate* would start a highway journey. During that haunting fjord cruise, I remembered old stories of terror and survival at sea. Inspired by another whirlpool near the Lofoten Islands, (and also by Samuel Coleridge) Edgar Alan Poe produced a story within a story titled *The Descent into the Maelstrom* in 1841. In it an old man reveals that he only appears old—"You suppose me a *very* old man," he says, "but I am not. It took less than a single day to change these hairs from a jetty black to white, to weaken my limbs, and to unstring my nerves." His ship was caught in the vortex. His companions died but the narrator survived, and described the whirlpool as a beautiful and awful phenomenon, that is, sublime. He held on to a barrel and was saved several hours later. Poe's tale is one of many dark tales of the North—stories of shipwrecks and survival. On *Pirate* we crossed the whirlpool in calm, so we could easily say, with Poe, the following:

> *When it is flood, the stream runs with a boisterous rapidity; but the roar of its impetuous ebb to the sea is scarce equaled by the loudest and most dreadful cataracts; the noise being heard several leagues off, and the vortices or pits are of such an extent and depth, that if a ship comes within its attraction, it is inevitably absorbed and carried down to the bottom, and there beat to pieces against the rocks; and when the water relaxes, the fragments thereof are thrown up again. But these intervals of tranquility are only at the turn of the ebb and flood, and in calm weather, and last but a quarter of an hour, its violence gradually returning. When the stream is most boisterous, and its fury heightened by a storm, it is dangerous to come within a Norway mile of it. Boats, yachts, and ships have been carried away by not guarding against it before they were within its reach.*

As the boat was hauled onto a Finnish truck (I had made the logistical arrangements ahead of time, crane, truck and all) in the rather forlorn city of Rognan, at the very end of the Saltenfjord, Christina and I followed the same route by bus. The bus took us to the north of Sweden and the frontier with Finland, through Lapland and the home of Santa Claus, and down again, now in Finland, to the town of Kokkola, on the Gulf of Bothnia.

As we proceeded along this route, the landscape changed, from the steep mountains of Norway through the undulating scape of Sweden, to the swampy forests of Finland (Suomi, the Finnish name for the country, means "swamp"). This saved us having to reach Finland from north of Norway by sea, a voyage that would have taken a year. The landscape of Finland was shaped by the relatively recent (in geological terms) recession of continental glaciers, some 10,000 years ago. The country has innumerable lakes and rivers, and innumerable offshore islands. Just as Norway is the most mountainous country in Europe, Finland comprises Europe's largest archipelago. The town of Kokkola, our destination, is home to the Yxpila Boat Yard where we would leave *Pirate* for work in the long winter months. Many of the workers and artisans at the yard once worked for Nautor in Pietarsaari, 30 miles to the south along the same coast, which is also home to Baltic Yachts.

The Yxpila Boat Yard is exceptional in its expertise and its cleanliness, and specializes in the refit of classic Swans. It was run by a man who would become a dear friend, Ola Hallman. We miss him very much today.

The refit program was extensive. It was performed to perfection. I present the program below and serial inspections by the foremost technical expert on classic Swans; I think it is a model of how to refit and maintain a yacht like *Pirate*.

RECOLLECTION

TECHNICAL

Swan 38-019 *Pirate*, Program of Restoration.
Inspected by Nautor and performed by the Yxpila Boat Yard in Kokkola, Finland.

Nov. 4, 2008. The yacht was on shore.
Yxpila Boat Yard. Inspection done by Mr. Lars Ström.

RIG

Boom is a replacement and appears to be in good condition. Pls indicate what needs particular checking/advice.

(*Owner informed that the boom was replaced in 1989 when he bought the yacht, and has been repaired and welded in 2000.*)

Corrosion on mast at lower end, and at aluminum cleat above deck. To prevent further corrosion it is suggested that:

- Mast butt is insulated from stainless mast shoe by putting an insulating washer under the mast, G-Plate or similar would be good
- A thin sheet of plastic inserted between mast wall and sides of shoe
- Take care that there are proper drain holes in the mast shoe to avoid having water standing there

- The aluminum cleat to be removed, and zinc chromate or similar put in the screw holes and under it when re-attaching

(*The yard decided to clean the mast lower end thoroughly, and paint it with Inerta epoxy, a very tough paint system specially formulated for sticking to the hulls of icebreakers, which are subject to very strong abrasion when forcing through thick ice. The same treatment was done at the mast cleat.*)

Sheaves at mast top

- The forward sheaves have been replaced with new ones having smooth grooves, the aft ones are original with grooves for wire/rope, recommended that the aft ones are also replaced as the halyards are now rope only. *(Aft sheaves replaced with new ones having smooth grooves)*

Standing rigging

- If higher tension wire means Dyform this is not recommended as the strands have sharp edges, which damage the sails. The standing rigging appears to be in good condition, and the Norseman terminals are of the new type meaning the rigging has already been replaced sometime.
- If the insurance specifies a maximum number of years after which the rigging has to be replaced this has to be obeyed. *(Owner confirmed that standing rigging was replaced 2003-2004.)*
- It is not recommended that leather be sewn over the spreader ends; this is likely to cause corrosion which is invisible. If sail protection is needed use PVC covers intended for this purpose.

INTERIOR

- The mast bulkhead vertical joints each side of the door opening can be felt through the surface veneers. This is not alarming, but suggests it is checked whether it is possible to fill the joints with glue.

BILGE

- The lifting lug is rusting, and should be treated to prevent this from getting worse. Corrosion protection paint compatible with galvanizing denoted IC 531 Zinc is recommended, the yard is aware of the product. Hull-keel joint shows no cracking

(Lifting lug was cleaned and painted)

ELECTRICAL

- Owner informed 31 Oct. by e-mail that after installation of the new engine the propeller shaft zinc is consumed rapidly. This indicates a leak in the electrical system, and needs to be investigated by a marine electrician.
- There is no bonding needed on Swans except for the lightning protection system connected to the keel. If it is preferred to install bonding, a proper system must include large, permanently connected outside zinc, but in any case the electrical leak has to be eliminated first.

PAINT JOB

- The entire topsides were filled and faired at the time of the visit with the aim of creating smooth surfaces.

  (Topsides, boottop and covestripes as well as deck GRP areas and steering pedestal were painted to a high standard.)
- Inspection of the mast while being dressed at Yxpila Boat Yard, June 1, 2009
- The lower end of the mast received epoxy treatment.
- There was one point of concern—the wire headstay had a sharp bend just below the upper end terminal, probably the result of the halyard having sometimes been wrapped around the furling section. Although there are no broken strands it is likely that this will cause the wire to fatigue, and the recommendation would be to replace the head stay before leaving the yard. *(The yard replaced the headstay.)*

FINAL INSPECTION, June 11th in the water

Here are the findings of the inspection with the yacht in the water, rigged and finally ready at Yxpila Boat Yard:

- The main boom and Hall boom vang are in good working order. The mainsheet arrangement is peculiar as it has a coarse/fine adjustment possibility.
- There was an earlier opportunity to inspect the mast when resting on supports while being dressed.
- The lower end of the mast has been cleaned and treated with epoxy for improved corrosion protection, and the same treatment to be given to the area close to the aluminum cleats on the mast.
- The aft halyard sheaves at the masthead have been replaced with new ones having a single groove.
- The running rigging has not been replaced.
- The stainless steel chafing pieces on the mast above and below the halyard exits have been removed, and the holes filled with mastic. Chafing pieces are required only with wire halyards.
- Spreader ends are wrapped with tape.
- The standing rigging is in good order; except that the headstay wire had a sharp bend just below the upper end terminal, and will be replaced. A new swaged lower end terminal is required from Reckmann.
- The electrical bilge pump plumbing was modified.
- The hull topsides, GRP deck surfaces, cockpit and steering pedestal have been painted.
- The interior has been varnished, and corroded screws replaced.
- Side windows have been replaced.
- The lifting lug in the bilge has been cleaned from rust and painted.
- A radar pole has been added on the aft deck.

Other comments:

- The genoa sheet cars were installed the wrong way on the tracks, the stoppers should be forward. According to YBY they will be turned.
- The latch for the aft hanging locker door opposite the head is not working properly, the spring needs replacement.
- The fire extinguisher in the aft cabin appears to be very small compared to European requirements, Please follow this up accordingly.

- The genoa sheet turning block bases do not have drain holes. Originally the bases were anodized, but have been painted white sometime. It should be checked whether the drain holes have been blocked.

Yxpila Boat Yard (YBY) has performed work upon request or/and in agreement with the owner of the yacht.

It is the owner's responsibility to follow up above-mentioned recommendations.

Possible disputes or claims shall be submitted to YBY by the owner.

OY Nautor AB(Nautor)has not been involved in any repairs, nor has Nautor any warranties/obligations with respect to above-mentioned repairs or/and modifications.

It was *Pirate*'s third refit under my command. It was also the best. How to describe the work in Finland? Efficient, clean, meticulous, precise. And all agreements were sealed with a handshake—the boat came out as new.

Black and gold: A shining hull after restoration in Finland.

12

The Shoals and Rocks of Finland

Parempi virsta väärään kuin vaaksa vaaraan.
Better a mile of detour than an inch of a dangerous way.

—Finnish proverb

Sailors do not frequent the High Coast of Sweden, and yet it is an enchanted area to explore. The High Coast, in the Ångermanland province of northeastern Sweden, is a UNESCO World Heritage site for its unique and highly scenic land and seascape, and its distinctly red granite cliffs and rocks. Due to a combined process of glaciation and glacial retreat stemming from the last Ice Age, the once-compacted land is now steeply moving on up. Technically, it boasts a 900-foot rise or 'rebound'. The area stretches over 50 sea miles from north to south.

In front of this coast, on the other side of the northernmost section of the Baltic Sea, there is the bleaker coast of Finland, shallower and a bit treacherous. The Finnish coast extends from Tornio at the Swedish frontier at the northernmost point of the Gulf of Bothnia, down the eastern side of the Gulf to about 61°N and then turns gently southeast and east along the northern shore of the Gulf of Finland to the Russian frontier, about 60°28'82"N, 27°45'86"E. Fifty miles off the southwest corner of the mainland lie the

Åland Islands. The Bay of Bothnia (in Finnish *Perämeri*) is the northernmost part of the Gulf by the same name, which is in turn the northern part of the Baltic Sea. Because the land is still rising after the weight of glaciers was removed, the bay will be a large freshwater lake within 2,000 years. The bay today is fed by several large rivers, and is relatively unaffected by tides, so it has low salinity, and it freezes each year for up to six months. Compared to other parts of the Baltic, it has little plant or animal life. It looks desolate, but has its own charm.

All these coasts and islands were *Pirate*'s playground during two adventuresome Nordic summers.

When I told Mitch Gibbons-Neff (then president of Sparkman & Stephens) that we planned to cruise in Finland, he voiced concern: "But it's all rocks," he exclaimed. As always with Mitch, he was half joking, and half warning. In fact, the waters of Finland, from north to south, are challenging, and the coast is full of rocks and skerries, with narrow channels in between. One has to navigate with extreme care, especially in the area known as the Quark.

In our cruise during the summer of 2009, three elements stood out: extraordinary landscapes, gracious and helpful sailors, and rocks! We sailed and motored from Kokkola, north of the Quark in the Gulf of Bothnia, to the High Coast of Sweden, through various channels in the Åland Islands and back up the west coast of Finland to Kokkola. *Pirate*'s base was the Yxpila Boat Yard and our base while she was refitted was the town of Kokkola, where a very pleasant couple hosted us at their B & B in the old part of town. That section of the city is one of the most cohesive and extensive areas of preserved wooden buildings in Finland. This "downtown" area used to be a district inhabited by the city's craftsmen and sailors, with small plots divided among several families.

The city of Kokkola was founded by the king of Sweden, Gustav II Adolf, in September, 1620. At the time of the city's founding, sailing ships navigated all the way to the city centre, where the Market Square is now located. Strong uplift along the Ostrobothnian coast has modified the landscape of the area over the centuries; the bottom of the sea keeps rising, as it "breathes" from the retreat of the glaciers. Standing in the Market Square today, all that reminds us of the former Kokkolalehti bay is a small channel, the Kaupunginsalmi narrows, with the 21st century sea-front now lying more than a kilometer away. Kokkola is four hours by train from Helsinki. Over the course of repeated visits in two years, I got to know the city well, even in winter which I found pleasant and not too dark, and during which I could walk over the frozen sea to where *Pirate*'s mooring usually was during the summer. When the coat of ice is more than 60 cm thick, even trucks and heavy equipment can move over it.

Of the 180,000 offshore islands of Finland, the Åland archipelago deserves special mention as a cruising area. Åland has 6,700 named islands and an additional 20,000 smaller islands and islets waiting for sailors to discover. Only 60 are inhabited, mostly in the summer months. The only city is Mariehamn, which we visited twice—once as part of a cruise-in-company organized by the North American Station of the Royal Scandinavian Yacht Clubs and the Nyländska Jaktklubben of Finland (NAS), in the mother ship—the Norwegian Galeas *Loyal*—and the second time just by ourselves on *Pirate*. Czar Alexander II, who gave the town its name, meaning "Marie's Harbor" after his wife, founded Mariehamn in 1861. There are only a few thousand residents in Mariehamn, yet the city receives more than a million visitors every year. In the summertime, the city is a lively place with cafes, museums, and restaurants. Always a port of excellent seafarers, today it displays the magnificent *Pommern*, a steel cargo ship (or windjammer) built in the early 20th century. Now moored outside the Maritime Museum in the western harbor of Mariehamn, the *Pommern* used to sail the oceans between England and Australia. Like the rest of Finland, Åland was historically caught in a vise between two empires, the Swedish and the Russian. Today Åland's autonomous status means that the island group has its own government, language and cultural policy (a good model for solving the Malvinas/Falklands dispute in the South Atlantic). Since 1921, Åland has had its own parliament as well as a representative in the Finnish national parliament.

After cruising along the Swedish High Coast with its good harbors, deep water, and enchanting islands, we arrived in Oregrund (whence we visited the university town of Uppsala and home of the great naturalist Linnaeus) and then set a course across the Sea of Åland to the city of Mariehamn. The shortest route is about 30 nautical miles over the open sea. Then a new adventure began. We traveled through a profusion of islands large and small. The Skiftet channel was the only larger expanse of open water we crossed. Its waters are deep, and, we were told, often visited by Russian submarines on the prowl.

Although there is plenty of room to maneuver in the channels in the Åland archipelago, we often had to dodge large cruise ships. Other times we enjoyed having a bay all to ourselves. Large parts of the archipelago are still unspoiled and the guest harbors still feel authentic. We stopped at our friends Lars and Norah Colliander's island, where we had a fine reception and charming stay, tied to rocks fore and aft, and then continued our nautical tour. A sailing round-trip is about 100 nautical miles. We experienced some strong winds and flat calms, and plenty of opportunity to practice precision navigation.

One calm morning in our circular summer cruise of the Northern Baltic Sea, while crossing from Finland to Sweden, we had a surprising encounter with a set—or rather a nest—of submerged rocks in the middle of the Baltic. The breeze was light, so we hit them at slow speed. We tried backing the boat whence she came, but hit again. It seemed there were rocks in all directions. We were floating, but surrounded by rocks not shown on the chart; we relied on a large-scale electronic chart when we should have monitored the depth on a more detailed chart. We anchored in the small clearing, lifted the floorboards and checked for any breach of the hull—luckily none was found. We called our friend Ola Hallman in Yxpila, Kokkola, who in turn called the Finnish Coast Guard. Some 30 minutes later a cutter arrived, stood half a mile away from us, and communicated in good English by VHF Radio. The Finnish cutter sent a diver equipped with lights and underwater communication, to inspect *Pirate*'s underbody. The officer on the cutter's deck relayed his reports. "Three points of impact" he reported. I paled in fear. Then he said "Correction: only cosmetic." We were much relieved. Only the bottom paint was scratched. At that point, the Finns instructed us to wait until they circled the area and found an exit channel, at which point they signaled us to follow. We were free again! Their parting words were funny, despite the ordeal. "These rocks are not on our charts. Would you like us to name them "Pirate Rocks"? I readily and thankfully agreed. And so *Pirate* left her mark in Finnish waters. As for the Finnish coasties, I can only restate my impression of all the Finnish people

Pirate in the Åland Archipelago: Lars Colliander's Island.

it has been my privilege to know: utter correctness and professionalism prevail.

While weather and wind kept us bound in harbors, we made new friends, and acquired some of the local knowledge that would prove key. Along the Swedish high coast we rendezvoused with other Swans from Kokkola, visited islands, and ate the favorite summer treat of the Swedes and Finns: waffles with whipped cream and strawberries.

The mantra we had been given by an experienced Finnish sailor, "stay inside the channel markers," became the first reflex when plotting a course or choosing a route.

With a 2.1 meter keel, we were limited to channels 2.3 meters or greater. This is a much longer story, but serves here as an introduction to our one small triumph. We successfully navigated the channels from the south into Vaasa, a charming university city midway up the coast of Finland.

At the lighthouse island, Kylmapihlaja, off Rauma, we met a fellow Swan 38 sailor who had taken a high-speed trip out to celebrate being in the same waters and who kindly counseled us on routes north to Kokkola. Throughout our cruise, we had heard that the channels up to Vaasa were "formidable," so we had planned to sail out to the east, bypass Vaasa via mid-Quark islands and then head up to Kokkola…the major problems with our plans were weather and time constraints: Twenty knots-plus from the wrong direction!

Our new sailor friend, Pekka Kuusniemi, suggested the channel route up to Vaasa, and that with care we should have no problem…and thus we entered the long chain of channels that alternated between seemingly open sea and tightly constrained zags that at times (via ranges) required radical right or left turns. We had been initiated into these channels on our first sail from Kokkola to Pietarsaari; it is an important skill in these waters to navigate by ranges, an acquired art form of navigation.

As we made our way to Vaasa, we saw sea birds and a striking amount of algae, sign of the changing temperature and perhaps the number of electrical generating plants that dominate the coast. The Finns like to blame the Russians for the pollution in the Baltic, but I think they contribute a significant amount themselves by the paper pulp factories that festoon the coast, provoking a rise in the temperature of the sea, and turning its brackish waters into a brown soupy mess.

We were able to sail part of the way, but were often under power. What was truly exhilarating was our entry into the main shipping channel for Vaasa—it is wide and was full of sailing boats—finally, wind, depth, and space to maneuver, and for a few hours we were able to play! By that time, large commercial ferries approaching quickly held less fear for us, and were part of the calculations. Also, the restaurants of Vaasa were a reward in themselves, as was the easy and hospitable mooring at the local yacht club.

The original plan was to sail in Finland during the summer of 2009 and then have the boat shipped to New England, from a port in the Baltic. It did not work as planned, as the Dutch company that was to ship *Pirate* to home waters changed both the dates and the course of the delivery, which would have placed our yacht in a southern US port during hurricane season, so we decided to postpone the delivery one more year. Then, during that year, we radically altered course: we made the decision to sell *Pirate* and leave her to a new owner in Nordic waters.

Christina and I did not regret having to abort the transport of the boat that year, or to winter *Pirate* once again in that lovely town, at the friendly Yxpila Boat Yard. The following summer we would try again, but with a different purpose, this time crossing over to Sweden, and then crossing Sweden itself on the Göta Canal, towards Denmark, whence she would be shipped on the Dutch freighter to Spain, for delivery to her new Finnish owner who wanted the boat in Spain.

A RECOLLECTION

By Christina Spellman

Why did I ask to join the first transatlantic, or for that matter the first delivery from Bermuda, or to sail thousands of miles onboard? I found Pirate *to be a boat with a noble spirit, one that invited adventure, while offering the strength to endure the elements.*

But what truly intrigued me were the opportunities to understand the sublime —the sea and weather, and the drama or calm they produced, enabled me to better understand a concept that I had struggled with in my work life. The beautiful, as in sunsets or misty fogs, was easier to understand; whereas the sublime, if Edmund Burke was correct, carries within it something different than the beautiful, an emotional charge that intensifies experience.

Heading to sea seemed to me to embody this charge. While any voyage might be all smooth seas and following winds, the greater probability was that our courage would be tested and we would work with the sea, the wind, and the strengths of the boat to make our passages safe and meaningful.

My apprenticeship to Pirate *included learning to be "pre-modern"—provisioning for a 30-day voyage without refrigeration had its challenges. Beer bread, a whole Proscuitto and plenty of bacalao were our solutions, as was the friendly advice of a butcher who suggested that we freeze the meats we ordered into a block in which the most likely to spoil would be first. We used this block in place of ice. By day 10, we still had marinated lamb stew! We were also pre-modern in that we learned to ration water, fuel, and energy in all forms: human, wind, mechanical, even inertia. Intriguing, if frustrating, were times when the engine refused to work, so we used sails and made port navigating as carefully as the navigators of old.*

It was during a storm, when repairing a fitting for the jib at the bow pulpit, that I understood Burke better and realized that the Hokusai 'great wave' print was not an artistic exaggeration.

Pirate *rewarded us for many years, creating the means for adventures, for cementing and discovering friendships, and for learning her secrets. With her we visited islands and ancient ruins, traversed canals in Europe, sailed the Western Ocean, and crossed the Arctic Circle. We never lacked confidence that she was equal to what we asked—while knowing that we were all part of the same team.*

As a boat, she embodied smart design, material strength, and a spirit that was welcoming. My understanding is that she continues to offer adventure, the safety of knowing she is adequate to the challenges of nature, and to be kind to the sailors who play with her.

* * *

CHRISTINA SPELLMAN is the Executive Director of The Mayday Fund. She is a member of the Ocean Cruising Club and the North American Station of the Royal Scandinavian Yacht Clubs and the Nyländska Jaktklubben. She was first mate, co-skipper, radio officer, provisioner, and cook during the many thousand ocean miles on *Pirate*.

13

THE IDEA OF SAILING

"Believe me, my young friend, there is nothing—absolutely nothing—half so much worth doing as simply messing about in boats."

—KENNETH GRAHAME

As I approach the end of this tale and so many recollections, I would like to share some thoughts on what, as a sailor, I have experienced and learned about "messing about in boats." Don't we all carry with us the fond memories of toys that we loved and cherished when we were young? A boat is a charismatic toy that keeps us young. A perfect model of one's cherished boat is such a toy, but so is the real boat herself. As I look at the model of *Pirate* (see Appendix) it prompts the following reflections.

The Unique and the General

The previous chapters comprise the story of a boat, but they are also sketches of a lifestyle. They are aspects of a mode of existence that to me has meant happiness. I offer them as distillates of the experience of being able to reflect on what I was doing, feeling, thinking. It is as if I were able to observe myself over my own shoulder.

Now if I turn all this on its head and view my actions from the perspective of the situations in which I was (and am still) enmeshed, then I engage in another exercise called sociology. From this perspective even the most private things we experience are part of a larger trend. In other words, the unique is a product of the general and prompts a few general reflections.

Land

From time immemorial, geography and climate determined the fate of people. For centuries what mattered were the ways in which the physical environment shaped different communities, and not the way in which those communities transformed their natural surroundings. That has been reversed. No modern nation-state or person can exist without a territory, even though so many things make frontiers porous or obsolete nowadays. That is a paradox: we all need somewhere to live but are increasingly capable of living anywhere.

Air

In 1833, the French historian Jules Michelet said that, without a geographical basis, the people who make history would be walking on air. Little did he know that so many of us would be in this century walking on air. Air traffic and air waves, the instantaneous transmission of information and funds, the ubiquity of telecast images, the telephone, GPS, WhatsApp, and so many other devices have de-territorialized humanity.

We imagine ourselves simultaneously in different times zones and geographies, so much so, that it is hard to picture anyone or anything that is fully wherever she or he or it happens to be, and not also somewhere else. The youth who ride the subways plugged to smart phones, those who eat and watch TV, those who work and dream of a vacation, those on water who want the mountains, and those on land who want the sea: there is no such things as a fully-committed presence. Whether we like it or not, we are all cosmopolitan in some measure. Attempts at retrieving "grounded" communities are a bit ludicrous, and often lethal. History and current events have shown the hideous face of those who assert a mystical bond between state and soil, religion and soil, or race and soil. As of this writing, some great nations are dead or dying, while other nations multiply like maggots in the corpse of their predecessors. We have lost the soil, and many don't like it. We walk on air. We cannot ground our beliefs, our commitments, our loves. And so we pitch our tents and flags on the oddest spots.

For those who look askance upon this cycle of ground and groundlessness, I submit something else. That also, since time immemorial there were those (no doubt in smaller numbers) whose lives were not determined by the soil, but by the exigencies of water, and especially the sea. The sea is every bit as demanding, perhaps more demanding, than the land, yet it precludes all roots and boundaries, and the sense of mine and thine.

To be sure, many nations have patrolled the seas, claimed "territorial waters," or even vast tracks of the oceans. Once upon a time, Britannia ruled the waves. But what community can grow on a parcel of ocean? Empires, not nations, have risen from the sea. All that nations can do is parade their colors—and their guns—on the watery ways, but must keep moving, like street walkers on a sidewalk. The sea makes the whole world a joint-stock place. Who has ever kissed the waters of his ancestors? Why isn't Nelson's monument off Cape Trafalgar itself, and not on that far-away pigeon-smudged square? Where are the signs inviting passers-by to pause, and remember, that "here lies sunken" the *Graf Spee*, the *Titanic*, the *Lusitania*, or Captain's Slocum's *Spray*?

We do know where many of them are "down there," but even while we sail above them, the feeling is too abstract. At sea we leave no mark.

But Water Everywhere

Imagine, for a moment, a guide to an ocean—not the pilot chart, but a brochure intended for the public. You could read an introduction to get a general picture of the place, even of its history. But there would be no description of everyday life. You could plan your route with the help of nautical charts. But which sea guide would dare suggest to you a touring program, or main excursions to "principal sights?" Also, there would be no "place to stay." All these essential components of a proper guide would be missing, for they require land—or at least a coastline. All marks are ultimately landmarks, and only landmarks can be visited. Land affords the regularity and replication that helps the tourist trade. The sea provides no such assurance. It is always different—and a changeable, abysmal place cannot be captured by a guide.

Only a great writer could evoke the watery element in its universality and multiplicity, and produce a single, definitive pamphlet, which is also a joke. James Joyce managed the task, with aqueous humor, in *Ulysses* (1914). What, he asked, did his main character, Bloom, admire in water?

> *"Its universality: its democratic equality and constancy*
> *to this nature in seeking its own level: its vastness*
> *in the ocean of Mercator's projection: its unplumbed*
> *profundity in the Sunda trench of the Pacific*
> *exceeding 8,000 fathoms: the restlessness of its*
> *waves and surface particles visiting in turn all*
> *points of its seaboard: the independence of its units:*
> *the variability of states of sea."*
> — James Joyce, *Ulysses* (New York: Vintage Books, 1966) pp. 671–672.

There is the impossible water-guide. Elusive, indistinct, universal, ubiquitous in space, ubiquitous in time, water permeates and signifies all things, their beginning and their end. In this immense medium we place tenuously an object that also moves. That object is a boat.

Object and Place

Even after the introduction of super high-tech hulls, foils, rigging and sails, the sailboat remains an almost perfect human (that is, artisanal) object: in the materials (no matter how exotic) used for its construction, in navigation; above all, in the way it is possessed and handled. Human effort and natural elements (hands, muscles, wind, and water) form a harmonious whole.

A sailboat is also a place in which work and pleasure are conjoined, in which simplicity rules, and in which social evil is generally absent—it is left behind, on shore. Time on a sailboat, no matter how short, is always time out, mostly quality time. Of all inanimate objects, a sailboat comes closest to a pet in that it is capable of accepting human care (and the emotions associated with care: love, concern, respect, tenderness). The small sailboat (that is the scale I am assuming here) is almost always "owner-operated," that is, the perfect artisanal object. In the days of wood, the sailboat was also frequently owner-made, manufactured (the myth of Pygmalion). Few other objects (houses, musical instruments) are as distinctly signed as boats. Sailboats are subjective objects—at the opposite pole to the other, alienated objects of modern nightmares—AI included.

Means and Ends

Boats are also epic. Epic objects are rare in these times, hence highly valued. Sailboats bear the traces of trajectories, of transitions: the transformation of nature into a responsive object, the husbandry of natural forces in its use, the passage between worlds. A sailboat is primarily a sequence of transformative acts and a site of passage. In boatbuilding, for instance, we witness the transformation of matter through various stages and episodes. Everything that has to do with sailboats implies and implicates stages and episodes. Everything is preparation. Building, commissioning, maintenance, repair, the planning of a passage or a race, the voyage, and the routines aboard form a braid of ceaseless transitions—stages and episodes.

Trajectories are often paradoxical. To the outsider, the ostensive goal seems paltry in relation to the expenditure of money, time, and effort that is required. The exercise is all the more paradoxical in an age of technological prowess, of speed and efficiency, in which any instrumental argument in favor of boating is condemned as hopelessly futile. Yet this paradox is undone in the practice of the sport of sailing, through a series of detours. A fusion takes place between ends and means. The means, as in all ritual, cancel the end. The trajectory becomes its own object. Routines are repeated, without the repetition ever turning into boring surfeit. In this, sailing becomes a reduced model of life: a complete round of life realized in a small area.

Freedom and Necessity

How come a life lived in very confined quarters appears as freedom? I can only give some tentative answers. One is that confinement on a sailboat is confinement in the middle of infinity—the ocean, the sky, the weather. Another reason is that, on a sailboat, survival depends on mastery. And to master one's own fate in a physical, total manner, is the closest we can come, in practice, to human autonomy. Freedom is not whim, but mastered necessity. The totalization of effort, focused on survival, distinguishes even the harshest conditions on a sailboat from the oppression of other total institutions. In these (schools, asylums, barracks, prisons) a callous social machinery turns persons into inmates, and processes them as matter to be used or transformed. Persons are objects managed by a staff. In the realm of boats such oppressive totalization belongs to the past, in the days of the slave ship and the man o'war. Its memory lingers in jest, as in the expression "galley slave." But today, all extraneous necessity—profit, transportation, food procurement—is gone from sailing. All that remains is inner necessity, freely chosen.

The ocean is the domain of the pirate, the adventurer, the vagabond, the old whaler, and the sportsman or woman whose abode is a ship. While the sea is defined by the freedom it affords, and means nature, non-society, openness and space, the ship on the contrary means confinement, necessity, closure and culture. The full sailor, the archetypical "pirate," lives in a peculiar nook between a sea which he or she uses to abolish all society, and a vessel that gives rise to a tightly controlled society.

Jules Verne—a yachtsman himself—understood this when he wrote about the submarine *Nautilus*, which he distinguished sharply from a merchant vessel. For cargo boats (those who take wheat from one port to another, and return loaded with cacao—the kind of boat I used to board when I was a teenager, like the sleek MV *Rio Lujan*, under the command of stern Captain Carabelli Montero, ploughing the seas between urbane Buenos Aires and the wild, African-looking Northeast of Brazil) move between precise ports of call. *Nautilus*, on the contrary, is totally transformed by the very enormity of her passage. Her voyage is all.

Roland Barthes noted the raptures of infinitude and confinement in the figure of a ship:

> *"[. . .]The ship may well be a symbol for departure; it is, at a deeper level, the emblem of closure. An inclination for ships always means the joy of perfectly enclosing oneself, of having at hand the greatest possible number of objects, and having at one's disposal an absolutely finite space. To like ships is first and foremost to like*

a house, a superlative one since it is unremittingly closed, and not at all vague sailings into the unknown: a ship is a habitat before being a means of transport. And sure enough, all the ships in Jules Verne are perfect cubby-holes, and the vastness of their circumnavigation further increase the bliss of their closure, the perfection of their inner humanity. The Nautilus, *in this regard, is the most desirable of all caves: the enjoyment of being enclosed reaches its paroxysm when, from the bosom of this unbroken inwardness, it is possible to watch, through a large windowpane, the outside vagueness of the waters, and thus define, in a single act, the inside by means of its opposite. Most ships in legend or fiction are, from this point of view, like the* Nautilus, *the theme of a cherished seclusion, for it is enough to present the ship as the habitat of man, for man immediately to organize there the enjoyment of a round, smooth universe, of which, in addition, a whole nautical morality makes him at once the god, the master and the owner."*

—Roland Barthes, *Mythologies*; Hill and Wang; New York; 1972; pp.66-67.

A true world cruiser is not after a domicile on land. His or her goals are only watery. The vessel is the only and baseless home: protection and interior surrounded by infinity. With the passing of the old Nantucket whaler, today's long-range cruiser is the only human left who takes the sea for her or his abode. Melville joins Verne in praising the voyage without end, and the boat as the strangest of homes.

"There is his home; there lies his business which a Noah's flood would not interrupt, though it overwhelmed all the millions in China. He lives on the sea, as prairie cocks in the prairie; he hides among the waves, he climbs them as chamois hunters climb the Alps. For years he knows not the land; so that when he comes to it at last, it smells like another world, more strangely than the moon would to an Earthsman. With the landless gull, that at sunset folds her wings and is rocked to sleep between billows; so at nightfall, the Nantucketer, out of sight of land, furls his sails, and lays him to his rest, while under his very pillow rush herds of walruses and whales."

—Herman Melville, *Moby Dick*; Signet Books; New York; 1961; pp.77-78.

Time and Space

The smallness and relative inefficiency of the sailboat produces a third paradox: it reverses the expectation of our state-of-the art means of transportation—airplane, car, bus, and train. The inefficiency of the sailboat increases space and re-qualifies time. Fourteen miles around an island, under sail, become a significant saga that may take five hours to accomplish—the time it takes for a modern jet to cross the continental United States. A modest bay becomes the universe; an archipelago an immense cosmos (as the Aegean realm was, no doubt, for the ancient Greeks). Yes, sailing re-qualifies time—undoing, in this sense, the wholesale disqualification of time produced by the industrial revolution and its post-industrial sequel.

Due to standardization and the improved means of transport, travel has lost most of its former sense of enchantment and adventure. What the sailboat—the cruising yacht in particular—affords is an epic, not just "efficiency." Her small-scale world gives us all the excitement of vast space-travel with the difference that we find it nearby. A journey of 50 miles surprises the sailor with an infinite variety of new vistas and unknown experiences. Sailing along, gunkholing, he or she meets adventurers, merchants, brigands, other captains and crews, and many more human types that no longer flit by as they would on a 70-mile car ride on a highway. Often he or she not only meets but gets to know them. Each different port, cove, city is a new world, with different customs, architectures, mores and moods. The conversations with a tugboat captain in Messina, with a sailing couple in Lepanto, with mechanics in Levkas, with a fisherman in Madeira gave me more information than reading a dozen modern travel books. To extract similar satisfactions from a large-area world, people travel not 50 but thousands of miles in cars and planes at great speeds. But what do these means give them in experience? Almost nothing. Often we travel thousands of miles to find the same kind of city or environment on which we have just turned our back—the same brands of merchandise against a slightly different backdrop.

A sailboat is capable of extracting very rewarding satisfactions from a small-scale world. At the same time, with a proper offshore yacht like *Pirate*, it is also possible to go around the terrestrial globe. This small, incredibly slow vehicle/home turns into a spaceship. The sailing experience reintroduces such outmoded dispositions as patience, the alternation of "strong" and "weak" moments (it is said that ocean cruising consists of long periods of boredom interrupted by short periods of terror) depending on the intensity of the wind, weather conditions, mishaps, and emergencies. It also favors the surprise. The magic of sailing in a disenchanted world of frequent travel consists in the almost miraculous provision of a long-forgotten third alternative to the business trip, on the one hand, and the vacation, on the other: sheer adventure, doing justice to the very small while embracing the very large as well. The excitement, and the sense of wonder after the accomplishment, are intense.

Life and Death

Life on a sailboat produces a different experience and awareness of the body—its power and its limits against the immensity of the sea. During the first transatlantic, when working on the foredeck in a storm, we realized that Katsushika Hokusai's print *Under the Wave off Kanagawa* is not an exaggeration. It is the indispensable presence of the body that binds pleasure and work in one bundle. The boundaries of this bundle—body/work/pleasure—are distinct and pristine. Death too is present, simple, and pristine. It is right there, like a familiar companion of every voyage, all around the boat. I often ponder on the simplicity of death at sea: for instance, on the precariousness of survival in many a sailing episode. I think, with Ishmael, that yes, there is death in this business of sailing: "…a speechlessly quick chaotic bundling of a man into Eternity. But what then? Methinks we have hugely mistaken this matter of Life and Death. Methinks that what they call my shadow here on earth is my true substance."–*Moby Dick*; p 53. Such is the metaphysics of the sea. Life is intense; death, familiar and concrete.

Past and Present

Some extreme situations today are mediated by our modern, disembodied technology. There are a series of inboard devices, such as AIS, EPIRBs, GPS, SSB, VHF, SAT phones, radar, and so on, that can summon the world to the rescue. Then, in emergencies, it is like an older era calling upon the future for help. In a rescue at sea, the modern world cancels the boating experience (as in all catastrophic terminations of a sea passage upon the rescue of the crew by a large ship). These moments of transition are charged with ambivalence, largely due to the fact that it is not assistance between equals that takes place (as it was yesteryear, or is imagined in the high-tech adventures of space travel in our own age). What takes place is the live enactment of the subordination of the past to the present—the 16th century calling on the 21st, as it were. Such transitions, albeit in less brutal form, are effected every time one comes back on shore after a passage. The old is twined with the new. The experience is neither traditional nor modern; it is beyond such distinctions.

The rescue of the solo sailor in distress, by plane or by a larger vessel, bears some similarity to the rescue of whales trapped in the ice. It is saving a (voluntarily) endangered species. Sailing is a constant shuttle between "then" and "now."

Silence and Noise

With the notable exception of some intrusive devices, the sailing experience is an experience of silence, or at least of nature's noise. Silence is not the absence of all noise but the cessation of mechanical noise, and the end of chatter. The noises that take over are those of surf, and wind, and that singular noise produced by the contact between the boat, the air, and the sea—the hissing of the wake, the howling of a gale, the clatter of halyards, and the raucous flapping of canvas. Animal noises are rare, with the exception of gulls and other marine birds in flight. Powerboats, on the other hand, are an altogether different species, to which noise—vibrant noise—is essential. Sailboats operate in a field of natural force; powerboats, and especially speed boats, in a field of mechanical violence.

There is an aesthetic of silence in sailboats. Powerboats are garrulous and cluttered with objects (as with the replication of the living room in the stateroom, which condemns the powerboater to time-in rather than time-out). The "scenes" at a powerboat dock are different from those at a sailboat dock. The former resemble the sights and sounds of the trailer park—a condensed reproduction of suburban promiscuity and the backyard barbecue, even in the case of multi-million dollar boats parked next to each other. Sailboats on the contrary seem to always long for the horizon, for the open sea. Powerboats don't seem to favor big open spaces. Sailboats are solitary and silent creatures made to roam the vast blue yonder.

Leisure and Sport

There are two aspects of sport: the spectacle and the practice. In other words, there are sports that we watch and sports that we practice. Over the last two or three decades, the social definition of legitimate sports has become wider, stylized, and very positive. The practice of sports is now considered a social good, accessible to people from all walks of life.

Nevertheless, different sports are favored, and practiced, by different sets of people. The popular strata prefer to engage in, and better watch, collective sports of confrontation: soccer, rugby, softball, basketball. As we move up the social ladder, and we begin to find those people that have a greater amount of what sociologists call "cultural capital," and the number of Ph.Ds or other professional degrees increases, as well as, of course, income, the practitioners of sports begin to play with elaborate "toys." The competitive relationship between adversaries in these sports is mediated by technological gadgets, by machines. With the possible exception of aviation—and, in the science-future, solar sailing—yachting remains the ultimate sport of the upper strata who want to play with challenging and complex toys. It is probably the only sport that easily blends the traditional with the new. It is at the very center of the new structure of demand, and of a shift in both the technology and the symbols of sports.

The new sports of "piloting" all sorts of craft with all the trappings of high technology (for example, ultra-light aircraft, underwater vehicles, gliders, experimental boats) attract the privileged sectors of youth. They offer hitherto unknown pleasures of acrobatic mobility, a sort of technical vertigo in both high- or low-energy versions. In them, adventure and youth are mixed with a high-tech ingredient.

The prestigious, avant-garde sports provide an escape from saturated time and space. They advance, literally, towards "new frontiers." They are in consonance with the ideology of innovation, the talk of "cutting edges," and new types of productivity that circulate in business, science, and technology circles. This type of sport offers adventure and emotion, shared in small, privileged groups.

In part, these developments correspond to the need to move the field of sports away from institutional forms that have become saturated and hidebound. But they also correspond to changes in other systems: the economic environment, the media, and the technologies. Thus, there are strong pressures from the side of business enterprises to find an individualized clientele, both very private and very solvent, capable of ordering and consuming refined, technologically sophisticated, and customized goods, long on value added and short in their lifespan.

These changes entail perverse byproducts. In sailing, as with most sports, the prevalence of the values of business and competition, the transformation of winners into celebrities, the acceptance of the market as something purely good, are accompanied by a decline in the value of the public interest or to the sailing community. High performers are not always good citizens, and the Corinthian[7] spirit is lost. Yet, except for some hotshot racers and professional teams, these negatives do not permeate the sport.

The Few and the Many

There is another perverse effect of sailing as a leisure activity regardless of whether or not it is competitive. The quest for freedom and adventure depends on a world that is neither totally administered nor crowded by too many people similarly inclined.

Sailing is subject to the same logic of self-defeat that haunts other modern pursuits of happiness. It is a simple sociological law, formulated as follows: The psychological satisfaction of using an object like a sailboat depends on the conditions in which it can be used, which will be strongly influenced by how many other people are using them. This factor, which is social in origin, may in the end be a more important influence on the satisfaction of sailing, than the characteristics of the sailboat as a charismatic toy. Conditions of use tend to deteriorate as use becomes more widespread.

As Henry James remarked of the tourists in his (more gentle) days, "You feel yourself at times in danger of thinking meanly of the human personality; numerosity, as it were, swallows up quality, and the perpetual sense of other elbows and knees

[7] In 19th century usage, "corinthian" meant profligate, or given to elegant dissipation. Later in the century the term was applied to the amateur yachtsmen, and it referred to the fellowship of those who love to crew on sailboats and help each other. In the U.S., that spirit of camaraderie among sailing amateurs is embodied in an organization that bears that very name. The Corinthians was founded in the 1930s, patterned after the Little Ship Club of England.

begets a yearning for the desert."[8] In my own case, numerosity begets a yearning for the shoreless sea.

World recessions, coupled with the shift in popular taste away from sailboats and more in the direction of runabouts and motorboats in general, has slowed down the proliferation of sailing craft upon some bodies of water. Nevertheless, it "ain't what it used to be," as any veteran world cruiser can tell you. Marinas are congested. Traffic in some ports is not only intense, but insane, for the waters are traversed by large contingents of the reckless and the silly on various types of craft.

A World Beyond

A few good boats and a few good sailors always move on, until they find bodies of water that are less encumbered by jet-skis, speedboats, family cruisers, and assorted stinkpots. Of course, remote islands are being readied with large fleets of charter boats, eager to receive a jet-hopping clientele. These tend to be the "picture-perfect" spots, not the more rugged or challenging areas that some sailors prefer, and which would scare most well-groomed consumers of packaged fun. The horror of hardship, the prospect of fear will keep the common consumers of leisure at bay. For them is the old nautical saying mentioned before: "He who would go to sea for pleasure would go to hell for a pastime." For those of us who seek fulfillment in an unencumbered world, the expanse of an ocean, faced from the deck of a well-tempered yacht, is a sublime place. With Ishmael we can say: "I love to sail forbidden seas and land on barbarous coasts."—from *Moby Dick*, page 26.

The wind sings in the rigging, the salt spray wets the face, *Pirate*'s lee rail is once again awash. The boat sails on. She crosses other boats, where kindred souls declare: "My boat, and the whole world." After one long passage, a second one is readied, and after the second, a third. The boat is but a speck in time and on the sea. Her passages however, with all other such passages, attempted or just dreamt, in all sorts of boats, form a continuous braid of hope, adventure, freedom, for ever and aye.

[8] Richard Howard, ed., *Henry James: Collected Travel Writings. Great Britain and America: English Hours, The American Scene, Other Travels*, New York: The Library of America, 1993.

14

The Final Cruise

Kemst þó hægt fari.
(You will reach your destination even though you travel slowly.)

—Icelandic proverb

Festina lente.
(Hasten slowly and you shall soon arrive.)

—Roman proverb

The Göta Canal, 100 NM long, connects the Baltic Sea and the Kattegat at the Swedish west coast. Almost 200 years old, the Canal starts at Söderköping near Sweden's east coast. It meanders through the countryside, past smaller lakes such as Roxen and Boren, farms and royal estates, before reaching Lake Vättern's eastern shore. Then from the western shore of Lake Vättern, via lakes Bottensjön and Viken, the canal winds its way to the village of Sjötorp at the east coast of Lake Vänern.

During this final cruise, *Pirate* sailed high above motorways—twice! Between the east coast and Vänern, the Canal passes through dozens of locks. The locks have to be managed by the crew on the boat, and couples alone have a hard time with the lines, so it is best to have at least three on board....

Sailing over the highway.

otherwise the Canal could live up to its reputation as "the divorce ditch." At the end it flows into the Trollhätte Canal. This second canal is 82 km long (44 NM), 10 km of which are artificial, the remainder being a natural waterway. The difference in water level between Lake Vänern and the sea is 44 meters (144 feet). This difference is achieved by six locks: one in Lilla Edet of 6 meters, four at Trollhättan of 32 meters total, and one at Brinkebergskulle of 6 meters These canals literally cut Sweden in half, and end on the West Coast in Gothenburg, a large cargo port and industrial center. It was home to Volvo cars (now a Chinese company) and to Saab (now defunct), the producer of cars and planes.

We spent the spring and summer of 2010 sailing from Kokkola in Finland to Sweden via the Göta Canal, and Fredrikstadt in Norway to Kalundborg in Denmark, where *Pirate* would be lifted onto a Seven Star transit ship—final destination: Palma,

The Göta Canal.

Mallorca. Leaving the Baltic was a bit melancholy because it would be our final sail aboard *Pirate*. We had sold her after 21 years of ocean sailing. Our last sail was a 1,500 NM cruise of all four Nordic countries: Finland, Sweden, Norway and Denmark, in the company of the new owner.

The cruise started in North Finland on a cold morning of May 22, 2010. There were growlers in the water when Harri Svahn, the new owner and I left the dock at Yxpila! After crossing over to the High Coast of Sweden and descending toward the Stockholm archipelago, we were joined by Christina, recently arrived from New York. The three of us crossed over along the Göta Canal—a process that took going up and down 58 locks, crossing the two large lakes, and a final stretch to Gothenburg.

We then went up the Western Swedish Coast to Norway (we had to leave the EU and re-enter) visiting the medieval city of Fredriskstad—with the largest congregation of Colin Archer double enders I have ever seen[9]—and then descended along the same coast towards Denmark, where we waited in the port of Kalundborg for the yacht to be transported to Spain. The new owner wished her to be Palma, where he had plans to cruise the Mediterranean.

The sail to Kalundborg through the Kattegat was raucous. Not only were the seas confused and choppy, but fast ferries crisscrossed the waters at great speed. We had to keep constant vigilance for traffic, with eyes scouting the hazy horizon one moment and looking at the screen for AIS warnings (Automatic Identification System, which tracks vessels at sea and is a valuable aid in avoiding collisions) the next moment. We were reefed as we entered the Kalundborg Fjord; we saw a landscape agricultural and green, where sailboats tacked across the main shipping channel, ferries plowed through. The Kalundborg Church and Radio Tower proved good navigational beacons. Yes, this was an industrial center, but it also was an old town that was historic and picturesque. On the island of Sjaelland, one is never far from the Vikings and their history.

We had a choice between tying up at the town's guest harbor, well-channeled and deep, or visiting the local yacht club on the western side of the large harbor entered through a channel that the charts indicated was 2.5 meters and the Pilot Book mentioned as 2 meters. As we had some uncertainty about the timing of the *Ankergrach*t, the transit ship, we opted for the Gisselore Yacht Club. This is not a harbor for deep-keeled boats, but with care it can take yachts with a maximum draft of six feet, and perhaps a little more.

What we could never have imagined was the generous welcome and hospitality we were given. Minutes after tying up, we were invited to the club's monthly supper and before long we were the objects of local curiosity. We were whisked off to visit the extraordinarily beautiful surrounding countryside and invited to homes so that we might learn the traditions that are still deeply held in the area. The citizens of Kalundborg are proud of their town and their culture, including the "industrial symbiosis,"

[9] The famous Norwegian naval architect built about 60 yachts, each to unique drawing, half ot them were double enders and the other half with counter sterns. They inspired designs by other architects around the world, from the Atkins, father and sons in the US, to the elder German Frers in Argentina. See *German Frers, Viajes, diseños, regatas*, Buenos Aires: Ediciones Letemendia, 2007.

they have developed for coordinating and reusing the energy that local industry consumes. The nearby island of Samso is a model of green sustainable agriculture.

Kalundborg is well served by trains and buses, so day trips to Copenhagen and the Roskilde Viking Ship Museum are easy. The club's harbormaster arranged a rental car for us and we received no end of insider tips on where and how to discover the region. For us, Kalundborg represented a powerful lesson learned; industry does not have to be ugly, but can actually be intriguing. We left the port with new friends and deep respect for the pragmatic environmentalism the Danes practice.

The American poet John Greenleaf Whittier composed a poem about Kalundborg's Church that involves a troll and a love story. In the preamble, he wrote, *Here is a wild tale of the North…of the fair island low lying off the pleasant Swedish shore, washed by the Baltic Sea and watched by Elsinore.* The hero of the poem must build *at Kalundborg by the sea, a church as stately as church may be.* We lay facing the church (it doubled as a fortress), which is indeed stately and hauntingly beautiful in first light!

Kalundborg's gift to *Pirate*'s crew was the new friendship of Ulrik and Suzanne Outzen, who graciously hosted us and with whom we continue to sail from time to time, on either side of the ocean that both separates and unites us.

When the transport ship arrived, *Pirate* was hoisted onto the *Ankergracht*'s deck by the ship's cranes. As the crane lifted *Pirate*, it seemed to us like the ascension of the wondrous vessel to another life, another destiny. We bid our trusted yacht a melancholy farewell, and flew back to the US. After 15 days, she arrived safely in Palma de Mallorca.The new owner wanted to rename her *Marhar*, and she would fly the Finnish flag. After three years he sold her to another Finn sailor, Henrik Resman, who fell in love with the boat and her story, and gave her back the original name. *Pirate* sails again in her original birthplace!

No better end to our enormous ocean cruises on *Pirate* over 20 years than the poetic vision of our truly last port of call, the Danish town of Kalundborg, from which we bid farewell to our magic carpet. For us old *Pirate*-mates the long episode was over. From my perspective, as I wrote this book, the adventures are braided into a wondrous dream. Our vessel, other boats, mates, people, and places dance in my mind as characters in a play, or figures in a haze. With the Bard we may say:

Our revels now are ended. These our actors,
As I foretold you, were all spirits and
Are melted into air, into thin air:
And, like the baseless fabric of this vision,
The cloud-capp'd towers, the gorgeous palaces,
The solemn temples, the great globe itself,
Yea, all which it inherit, shall dissolve
And, like this insubstantial pageant faded,
Leave not a rack behind. We are such stuff
As dreams are made on, and our little life
Is rounded with a sleep.
—William Shakespeare, from *The Tempest,* Act 4 Scene 1.

Sailing has changed, and so has the world surrounding it. They will continue to change. I could have named this book, like Stefan Zweig, "the world of yesterday"—things comprehensible yesterday, and that tomorrow will never know. I am not nostalgic. We had too much fun for that. I just wished to present some pictures of that fun, like images in an exhibition.

15

From One Classic to the Next

We use the word "classics" for those books
that are treasured by those who have read and loved them;
but they are treasured no less by those
who have the luck to read them for the first time
in the best conditions to enjoy them.

—Italo Calvino

As to a Classic Yacht, I know one when I see it.

—A Past Commodore of the
Classic Yacht Club of America

When we left *Pirate* in Finland (via Spain) I asked myself why? Christina asked the same question. We had a boat made for a lifetime. How can you be both determined and puzzled at the same time? I *knew* it was the right thing to do, but had not managed to articulate the reasons. When people questioned me, my only answer was a shrug. Now, at the end of this book, I think I can provide something resembling a rationale. Now I know that self-knowledge is a knowledge that comes after, just as adventure is the opposite: a vision of the possible that comes before. Enlightenment is belated and retrospective. What follows are the reconstructed reasons for doing what at the time I just felt compelled to do.

I had the the feeling that our years on the boat, and the many miles we sailed, and the oceans we crossed, had arrived at a point of completion. Given our age and condition, *Pirate* had given us all we wished from her, and then some more. Completion in this sense meant accomplishment, reaching a sort of existential destination, in short, a fulfillment. The time had come to let her go—but not in just any way, to anyone, in any place.

Completion, or closure, meant also homecoming for the boat herself. We had her restored in Finland, where she was born, in a place where classic Swans were produced, and surrounded by people who had shaped her hull and built her spars in 1974. When my first attempt to ship the restored *Pirate* back to America failed because of delays in schedule, I had the sense that the mishap was a sign, a sort of secret message. A voice whispered in my ear: "she wants to stay."

My conditions were firm. If she were to stay, *Pirate* would only be sold to a Finn, fly the Finnish flag, and be kept in the waters of her birth. More than a sale—I explained to my friend Ola Hallman, who would act as broker—it should be a transfer, a new rite of passage. Like Odysseus, *Pirate* had finally arrived in Ithaca—a voyager come home at last, rich not with treasure but with baggage of adventure and tales to tell. Homecoming and fulfillment: that is how Homer's epic poem ends.

All this occurred in a sequence that seemed foreordained. I had the impression that we had been under the spell of a force stronger than any god we may conventionally worship, hence the reference to ancient Greece. To the Greeks, all their gods, including Zeus, must bow to the mysterious power of fate, the strongest force of all, and maybe the oldest. The sale of *Pirate* was perhaps an unconscious return to a plan that had been laid out beforehand.

And that is how it happened. After a small interlude in the Mediterranean under her new owner, *Pirate* returned to Finland. She changed hands once more, to another Finn sailor, as if looking for a more perfect master.

Christina and I went back to America. As sailors we were bereft. As opposed to *Pirate*'s, our own homecoming was incomplete. Our old boat had attained completion, but how about us? It's one thing to end one's voyage on this earth, like Abraham, "sated with life," but a very different thing to survive completion. I felt the dread of having to lead an afterlife that, to many people, is what retirement means. How would we keep sailing, and on what? But all ends are new beginnings, and so a search began.

This time instead of searching forward, we searched back. We longed for completion with a type of boat that was traditional and proven, something that L. Francis Herreshoff called "compleat." For Herreshoff the words "classic" and "compleat" meant "romantic," and I think that is what we wanted: a boat beautiful and old-fashioned, a boat where we could have peace and freedom, away from gadgets and easy comforts, and relying mostly on the old arts of seamanship. He wrote: "When a thing is out of the usual and pleasing to contemplate, it is romantic. When an object is nicely proportioned and has retained some well-proven ancient quality, it is romantic looking. I suppose to a sailor a romantic vessel is one that looks like a good sea boat, one which has good sheer and nicely proportioned ends: in short, a vessel that he falls in love with at first sight."[10] Late in life, we were looking for romance in a new old boat.

From our *Pirate* experience we brought this viewpoint to the search: that a classic boat has to be "right," especially when she is going to be used as she was intended and sailed a lot, as well as occasionally raced. She would be sailed daily, especially on evening sails in Buzzards and Narragansett bays, and from time to time raced offshore and inshore, from Eggemoggin Reach in Maine, to Halifax in Nova Scotia, and to Bermuda as well. That was the idea, and nothing fitted the program better than a Concordia yawl. We had found our target.

When *Pirate* was first launched in 1974, she was a modern, competitive racer-cruiser, and very much state of the art. The original brochure stated: *The smallest of the Swan range, she is the one that can comfortably be handled by a man-and-wife crew, yet give the same thoroughbred performance. The '38' owner needs neither a large family nor a bevy of friends to take her sailing. Not that she can't accommodate them when they do turn up. She can sleep, wine and dine eight in great comfort.* The Swan 38 was designed to the (imperfect) International Offshore Rule, in the early, saner days of that rule,

[10] L. Francis Herreshoff, *The Compleat Cruiser. The Art, Practice, and Enjoyment of Boating* (New York: Sheridan House, 1956, reprinted 1994) p.97.

and won many races in her prime. Many other boats in that category, especially later in the days of the IOR, became superannuated, and as such were discarded without a second thought.

When we acquired *Pirate*, she was sixteen years of age, but as we sailed her year after year, and before our very eyes, she did not get old. Instead, she became a classic. The distinction is crucial. A classic—painting, music composition, car, book, or boat—is an object that is more than an object, because it has a soul. In other words, a classic establishes the very norms by which it must be judged. It proposes a game for us to play—a game at which the classic creature is unsurpassed. It never ceases to express what it really means. That explains why *The Birth of Venus* by Botticelli, *The Pastoral Symphony* by Beethoven, *Don Quixote* by Cervantes, the Ferrari Barchetta by Pininfarina, or the Swan 38 by Sparkman & Stephens, do not grow old.

Some classic objects are born classic; others become so, like a chrysalis turns into a butterfly. The latter case is a metamorphosis that happened with the Sparkman & Stephens Swans[11], and that we witnessed with *Pirate*. Our new search was for the former type of classic yacht: a boat born classic, and designed for completion, not competition, from the very start. Both types of classic boats have fulfilled the cycle of their existence, beyond which they do not reach. If well maintained, they remain in that state of completion, in principle, "for ever." They have attained in their own manner an inner completion within their watery life, as they followed the (today naïve) clarity of their simple purpose.

That is not the case for those who strive for a different kind of self-perfection in the acquisition of new objects, new records of performance, and new forms of competition. They could indeed be tired of life but not sated with life, in the sense of the completion of the course of life. For them perfectibility is limitless. The more objects are invented, differentiated and diversified, the more trivial becomes the fraction that an individual—as a passive recipient or an active creator—could encompass in the course of a life. You can be certain that after you are gone, a better model of car will hit the market, ever faster boats will race, and artificial intelligence will make life ever

[11] See Matteo Salamon, *S&S Swan. A Legend* (Florence: Viol D'Art, 2016)

more perfectible. But there is no guarantee that by the end point of an individual's life, which is always "accidental" in its term, this was a meaningful conclusion. The end is just an accident for a trivial individual caught in the perpetual race of perfection. These are words that I recall from Max Weber's indictment of modernity. (Max Weber was a German philosopher, jurist, and political economist considered a founder father of modern sociology.) Our search for a classic boat born "compleat" was meant as an antidote to the rat race—a way to graciously complete our own life. She would be a boat that came already "sated" and that would be in turn the site of our own satiety.

In both the case of a "born classic" or an "evolved classic," the passage of time, and the struggle against the passage of time, is perhaps the most important factor. Time is change, and change is irreversible. Nevertheless, a classic—boat, car, house, and book—resists the inexorable, unavoidable, and irreversible passage of time in various and interesting ways. One has to maintain the object, and especially the practices around the object, in their integrity, albeit with concessions—big and small—to the new contexts in which time throws them. Classic regattas are a case in point. In them, both the boats and the venue appear in a present that is also the past. The modes of this nearly impossible quest to balance present and past are several, and they range from the sublime to the ridiculous. Classic boats, like old properties, are historic objects, but they are also alive—a condition that is more difficult to attain with other historic objects, like mansions and houses, that seem to be almost irremediably condemned to sheer museology, or the axe. With classic boats, as with historic properties, there are several paths to follow in their treatment and their use. I will list the four principal ones.

- Conservation focuses on the maintenance and repair of existing historic materials, and on the retention of the vessel's form as she has evolved over time.
- Rehabilitation acknowledges the need to alter or add to a classic boat to meet continuing or changing uses, while retaining her historic character.
- Restoration presents a boat at a particular period of time in her history, while removing evidence of other periods. This comes closest to museology.
- Reconstruction re-creates vanished or non-surviving portions, or the entire structure of a boat, sometimes starting from a few original parts or just the

drawings. It may be done for interpretive purposes but also to use the vessel in many ways. The reconstruction of *The Coronet* is one example. Another, different example, is the building of the Olsevar, or Oselvar, a small wooden rowing boat built traditionally and used along the west coast of Norway. The Oselvar is a clinker built boat with thin, very wide planks. Almost all parts of an Oselvar are made of pine, with only the keel of oak. A newly minted Oselvar is as genuine as an old one. A third interesting example is the new boats built in the "spirit of tradition." In fact, all these boats in the fourth instance are simulacra of the historic past—what the Chinese call "authentic reproductions."

The first three treatments of classics are sometimes kissing cousins, sometimes fighting cousins. The fourth, especially the often-spectacular boats built in the spirit of tradition, is a different species altogether.

Our search became more focused. We wanted a classic, born a classic or at least with a longer classic pedigree than good old *Pirate*, and also something that at first blush seemed impossible: a boat very different from *Pirate* and yet very similar too. Different in materials, shape, looks below decks and above. Similar in being ocean capable, a boat as comfortable inshore as offshore, a cruiser that could race (in the proper context), similar in size, and similar in the ability to spring a surprise. Just as *Pirate* won three Bermuda Races when she was considered a small old boat, Concordia wooden yawls have won the Newport Bermuda Race twice, the Maryland-based Annapolis Race, Cowes Week, the Marblehead to Halifax Race and many others, racing under CCA, IOR and IMC ratings. And they were designed without regard to the rating rules!

In the 21st century, the Swan 38 would be considered superannuated in most races. In the eyes of a modern designer, looking at a wooden boat and her displacement/length ratio, the low-aspect sail plan, and a full keel, a wooden sloop or yawl like a Concordia, would be dismissed as a dog—pretty as she may be. And yet, two modern designers of world renown whom I know, German Frers and Juan Kouyoumdjian, own, restore, and lovingly sail, wooden boats.

These facts intrigued me, and with the strong endorsement of Christina, I started exploring the Concordia yawls that were on the market in 2011. We looked at seven such vessels, and chose the one that seemed best tested, best maintained, and most robust; her owner, John Melvin, had taken her offshore, and did very well in modern races. Under Melvin, in the Newport to Bermuda race, she could boast: 2nd in class in 2006, and 4th in class in 2008. In 2006 she also won her class in the Block Island Race. Under her first and second owners, she came first in class in the Newport to Bermuda Race in 1968, sailed to Norway in 1969, and did very well in the next two decades. At the other end of the spectrum, in 2009 she won the "Venerable Cooks Award" in the Marblehead to Halifax race, as well as in the 2010 Bermuda Race. Her name was *Westray*, and she is our present magic carpet, a watery home away from home, and a direct connection to a tradition of seamanship that is fading but wondrous.

If you look at the numbers, and on paper, the Swan 38 and the Concordia 39 are almost twins. If you experience them in real life, they are enormously different. One is driven by the genoa, as by the IOR specifications. A large, low-aspect mainsail drives the other hull. One is a sloop; the other a yawl whose mizzen seems a mere afterthought, or a stick to hang the laundry on, until you learn her tricks in picking up a mooring without engine power, or backing the boat down without the help of a prop, or adding speed in a race, in the spectacular deployment of a mizzen staysail on a broad reach. The staysail adds both speed and stability on a specific point of sail, and adds beauty to the sight of the wooden boat on the water. On the other hand, back at the mooring, putting the sail cover on the mizzen boom requires some gymnastics and a tall person in the crew. And in a fresh breeze or near gale, you can forget the mainsail and cruise under jib and jigger alone, as if it were a balmy afternoon.

Besides, fiberglass, aluminum and steel sound and feel different than the various woods that compose a traditional boat: mahogany, oak, pine, and locust. When these different elements "speak," you listen. The pace, the tracking, the momentum, are all different, and each requiring different skills in the middle of the sea.

Below deck, the space is more restricted in our wooden yawl than in the Swan. However, after our "pre-modern" experiences in the Swan, we have easily accommodated to the more primitive features of the Concordia. We have kept the alcohol 2-burner stove and take it into consideration when we provision for a cruise or a

The classic Concordia yawl, *Westray*. Photo credit: Tyler Fields

race—pre-cooked meals are a must. We appreciate the way stowing stove boards was so carefully thought out. And there are singular delights in the cozy-cabin feel of the Concordia, notably the Pullman berths, the settees with triangular pillows, and the generously sized head, to say nothing of the wood-burning heating stove.

But in the difference you also find similarity: a classic Swan and a Concordia were each designed by a genius at his trade, who loved to sail the boats they drew, and sailed them to perfection, and were attentive to every little detail—never superfluous, always simple and just essential. Boats designed by maestros, built by artisans, to be sailed by all-around sailors.

Here, as a bookend, I like to present in a colorful chart with cold numbers some of their similarities:

Performance Comparison of the S&S Swan 38 sloop *Pirate* and the Concordia 39′ yawl *Westray*.

Top of Form

LOA	Concordia Yawl	39.83
	Swan 38	38.25
LWL	Concordia Yawl	28.5
	Swan 38	28.71
Beam	Concordia Yawl	10.25
	Swan 38	11.55
Displacement	Concordia Yawl	18000
	Swan 38	18300
Sail Area	Concordia Yawl	650
	Swan 38	686
Capsize Ratio	Concordia Yawl	1.56
	Swan 38	1.75
Hull Speed	Concordia Yawl	7.15
	Swan 38	7.18
Sail Area to Displacement	Concordia Yawl	15.14
	Swan 38	15.81
Displacement to LWL	Concordia Yawl	347
	Swan 38	345
LWL to Beam	Concordia Yawl	2.78
	Swan 38	2.49
Motion Comfort	Concordia Yawl	38.99
	Swan 38	34.16

As to performance, on our Concordia we experienced the full range, just as we did on our Swan, from slow to fast, winning and losing races, but always having fun. As a parting observation, I wish to note that both boats turn heads and have cult-like followings. The Swan and the Concordia have been welcomed in every harbor, and often given pride of place.

WESTRAY RACING RECORD 2018

Camden Classic Race

Second

Eggemoggin Reach Regatta

Classic Yachts, Division B

Second

Marblehead Corinthian Classic Yacht Regatta

Classic Wood Spinnaker

Second

Marblehead Corinthian Classic Yacht Regatta

Concordia Class

First

Padanaram 80th Concordia Rendezvous

Spinnaker Division

First

Concordian Trophy

Best Racing Record 2018

I'd like to end this book with a snatch of poetry from the repertoire of a quintessential member of the Cruising Club of America: John Parkinson, Jr. Parkinson was the first master of the well-known Concordia yawl, *Winnie of Bourne*, which he sailed far and wide. My thanks to Stephen Ballentine of Cataumet, Massachussets, for showing me *Yarns for Davy Jones*; Archon: 1966, p.134, a rare and fascinating book.

When the great Recorder puts a mark against your name,
It isn't if you won or lost, but how you played the game.

—John Parkinson, Jr.

Appendix

The World in the Model: *Pirate* Redux

Marine artist Luca Ferron joined the braid of dream and adventure when he set out to reproduce *Pirate* in miniature, down to the smallest details on deck and below. He likes to quote an Arabic proverb that portrays this saga in scale 1:20. *"No track has ever led a caravan to a mirage, rather the mirage set the caravan in motion."* I like to call Luca the Leonardo Da Vinci of model builders, half in jest. We were introduced by Matteo Salamon, the enthusiastic organizer and editor of the S&S Swan Asociation. So *Pirate* was born again, this time as a woundrous toy. Bit by bit, step by step, detail by detail, from the hull to the interior, cleats, winches, and spars, and following the original plans from S&S, the artist manufactured a new *Pirate*. It took five years. The result is stunning.

Five photos showing the progress of the model and the result.

PIRATE
NEW YORK

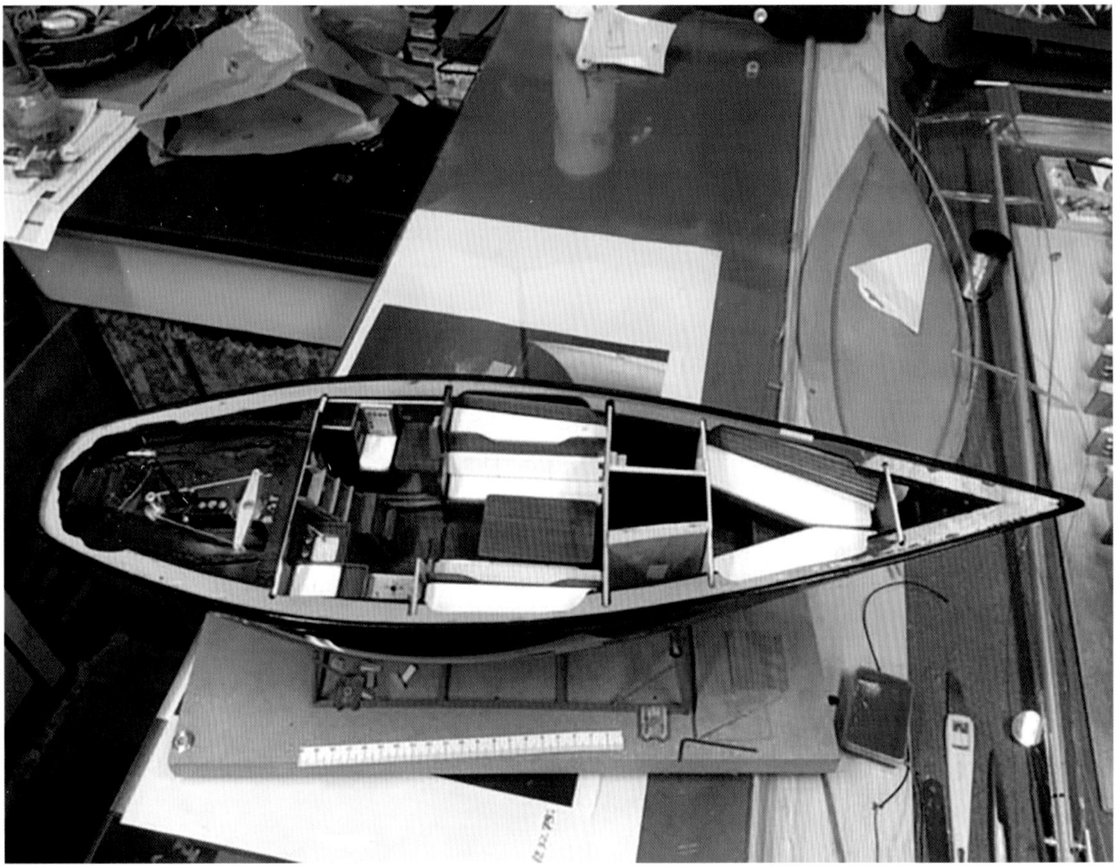

THE END